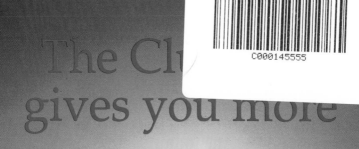

The Club
gives you more

C000145555

more Club sites . . . more Certificated Locations
. . . more services . . . more information

For more details of Club membership call us
FREE on 0800 52 11 61

THE CARAVAN CLUB

IT'S SO MUCH BETTER TO BELONG

THE CARAVANNER'S HANDBOOK

'an exhaustive but easy-to-read guide by an experienced caravanner'
Practical Caravan

'Solid, down-to-earth information and advice on all aspects of caravanning... Well worthwhile'
Good Motoring

'a very worthwhile investment, particularly for beginners, but also for many older hands'
En Route

'153 pages of good sense... with dozens of useful hints and tips... very good value'
Volkswagen Audi Car

'an informative and entertaining read'
Caravan Magazine

Now in its fourth edition, this hugely popular handbook has been fully updated to provide an immensely interesting and useful asset to all members of the caravanning world, whether newcomers or seasoned hands.

Drawing on a lifetime's experience of caravanning, John Marchmont manages to combine a wealth of useful tips and information with a lively and highly readable style. His great love and enthusiasm for caravanning shine through as he humorously recounts experiences that would quickly deter the faint-hearted.

But, if it's practical, down-to-earth advice you want, you'll find it all here, including:

- Choosing a caravan
- Towing, loading and hitching up
- Reversing and manoeuvring
- Equipment and accessories
- Water, gas, electricity and sanitation
- Furnishing, maintenance and security
- Driving abroad
- Caravanning clubs
- Insurance.

A fun and inspirational read for all those considering caravanning for the first time and an essential source of up-to-date information for all those already smitten, *The Caravanner's Handbook* is an indispensable guide.

Don't hitch up without it!

THE CARAVANNER'S HANDBOOK

About the Author

John Marchmont, married with four grown-up children, is a retired driving instructor in his native Nottinghamshire. A member of the Institute of Advanced Motorists, he is one of the comparatively few members to hold the Institute's certificate for caravan and trailer handling. He and his wife Mary (also an IAM member) have been keen caravanners for many years.

He remembers being taken by his parents to Norfolk on his first caravan holiday in 1932. The van concerned more closely resembled a mobile garden shed and bore little similarity to the luxury caravans of today.

THE
CARAVANNER'S
HANDBOOK

Fourth Edition

A lighthearted but most informative book designed to explain to beginners some of the basic facts they should know about the subject and perhaps even provide a few hints for the 'Elder Statesmen'.

John Marchmont

IN ASSOCIATION WITH

Although there are as many female caravanners as male, the male pronoun has been used largely throughout this book. This avoids cumbersome and repetitive phraseology and no discrimination, prejudice or bias is intended.

Whilst this book was compiled with the assistance of the National Caravan Council, the views expressed in it are solely those of the author.

First published in 1986
Second edition published in 1990
Third edition published in 1991
This fourth edition published in 1993

Kogan Page Limited
120 Pentonville Road
London N1 9JN

British Library Cataloguing in Publication Data

A CIP record for this book is available from the British Library.

ISBN 0-7494-0936-3

Typeset by CG Graphic Services, Aylesbury
Printed in England by Clays Ltd, St Ives plc

Contents

Foreword

Like many others, I used to be 'anti-caravans', not only when they were on the road but on the various caravan parks up and down the country. I then read the first edition of *The Caravanner's Handbook* by John Marchmont and thoroughly enjoyed its contents. It certainly changed my views, and in fact the IAM now conducts an Advanced Caravan Towing test for its members.

This fourth edition is now fully up to date and is written in a lighthearted but informative way. It will help the novice caravanner to take up caravanning successfully and enjoy the freedom of taking part of your home with you.

There are excellent chapters on the actual towing procedure, reversing and manoeuvring and general hints. You will also find useful sections on camping sites in the UK and in Europe, and on motor caravans, as well as a whole range of other important topics.

This book will certainly assist and improve your towing skills, making you a safe and considerate caravanner and so creating a better relationship between the car driver and the caravanner.

Ted Clements MBE
Chief Examiner
Institute of Advanced Motorists

Acknowledgements

I am deeply indebted to the technical officers of both the National Caravan Council and the Caravan Club, and to the Information Officer of the Camping and Caravanning Club, who devoted much time and effort in helping me to ensure the accuracy of this book. I also owe much to the various caravan publications whose information and material I have plundered shamelessly.

I am grateful to the various accessory manufacturers who have readily provided information, and in many cases, samples of their products. Also to those who have taken advertising space in the book.

Last, but certainly not least, my thanks to my wife (Herself) for her unfailing encouragement and help, and for the pleasure of her company on so many caravanning expeditions.

JCM

Introduction

The Caravanner's Handbook starts here! Don't skip this part, just because it's called the 'Introduction'. If it wasn't relevant it wouldn't be included; anyway you've paid for the whole book so you might as well read it all.

The book is designed to help the novice caravanner to decide how to take the plunge, and to guide him or her through the maze of facts on how, what, when, why and how much.

It is also aimed at those who might have been caravanning for some while but still need information. Particularly I have tried to deal simply with the thorny problem of reversing and manoeuvring generally. One so often sees a business-like looking outfit arrive at a site (perhaps even having been towed on and off a ferry and through continental towns) only for the embarrassed driver to fail miserably when it comes to the simple matter of slipping the van into the allocated pitch, shunting back and forth looking miserable, while the other occupants run to and fro flapping their arms.

There is a wealth of advice and information on caravanning available in various commercial magazines and also from the Caravan Club and the Camping and Caravanning Club magazines and publications. The commercial magazines are *Caravan, Caravan Life, Practical Caravan* and *Caravan Answers*. These are all in magazine format and each contains a wealth of caravan-related articles on sites, van prices and reviews, new accessories and advertisements.

The most recent arrival among magazines is a new title – *Caravanning DIY*. This will appear in spring and autumn and contain detailed articles and illustrations of many simple and not so simple jobs which the caravanner of average ability can carry out himself. It is available from the publishers of *Caravan Life*.

Another addition to the printed scene is *What Caravan?* which is an absolute must for anyone contemplating joining the growing ranks of caravanners. This is in book format, much the same size and shape as the book which you are reading now. It contains buying guides for new and second-

hand vans, what to look for when buying second-hand, towing weights of caravans and a guide to car towing weights. There is also a useful section containing names and addresses of clubs, caravan manufacturers and relevant organisations.

All these publications are extremely helpful to the caravanner or would-be caravanner, and *What Caravan?* is virtually indispensable to anyone getting into caravanning for the first time.

14

Everything in this book can be found elsewhere with a little effort, but I have tried to collate a quantity of useful information, and draw on my own experience of many enjoyable years of caravanning, both here and abroad. The result will, I hope, help new caravanners and old hands alike to better understand and enjoy what is really more than a hobby, rather a way of life.

My family got into caravanning well over 25 years ago as 'failed campers' (and we are not alone in this category, I suspect). It started when, on the spur of the moment, we elected to go to the South of France. Not having the resources to finance a stay in a hotel for two adults and four children, we decided we would camp. Obviously!

Never having done so before was no deterrent to an idiot with my initiative. We borrowed a frame tent of vaguely defined dimensions, plus two small pup tents for our two boys. Our kind friends also lent us kitchen and cooking gear, and it was all handed over at a brief ceremony during which I enquired how one erected the tent. We were assured that once we had the poles sorted and the frame assembled it was all downhill from there. No problem!

So, with all this gear on the roof, the boot full of luggage and the car full of family we set off for St Raphael. In August! In those days there were no autoroutes, and we slogged on down the N7, getting hotter and hotter. We attempted far too much, of course, and on the second day we arrived at the sunbaked Riviera having travelled too far without stops. We were hopelessly dehydrated, and I had a crippling, monotonously pounding headache. The kids had thrown up at 20-mile intervals, and Herself had stopped communication with the outside world a couple of hours previously, but we had *arrived*! Monsieur showed us to our allotted pitch and left us.

I stood, swaying, and considered the mountain of gear atop the car. I thought about having to unload it all, sort it out and assemble it before I could crawl into bed and die in some sort of comfort. We were all tired, bemused and speechless. I then became aware of the unwavering gaze of our nearest neighbour.

On the next pitch stood a touring caravan, in the doorway of which loomed a lady of Wagnerian proportions, her hair

screwed up into an uncompromising bun. Her forearms and formidable bosom rested on the lower half of the stable door. Insulated by now from most feelings of normality, I watched aghast as she opened the door, descended, and bore majestically towards us like a galleon in a fair wind. The thought that she might be about to address me in German was the final straw. My head felt as if it was about to fall off anyway, and as she drew nearer I was seized briefly by an impulse to curl up on the ground, a gibbering wreck. She advanced until her face was about twelve inches from mine, halted, and then in the wondrously reassuring patois of the Nottinghamshire coalfields enquired, 'Should yer like a cuppa tea duck?'

From then on things briefly improved. It couldn't have been more than a couple of hours or so after dark before we had the tent poles sussed out, and we settled in. For two or three days we swam, ate, drank and loafed in the sunshine.

Then the Mistral struck! It blew and it rained. It rained stair rods for two whole days. The campsite – a pleasant, sloping, shrub-planted place with numerous gravel paths – became a sea of mud. The paths disappeared and several cubic yards of gravel washed down into the main road.

We sat for two days – Herself and I, plus two small boys and two small girls in this horrible wet tent. Damp and filthy, and thoroughly fed up, I played Monopoly, battleships and I-spy through clenched teeth.

So there, on that soggy foreign field, was recruited another caravanner. As I sat there with my clothes sticking to me, with everything potentially edible covered in mud, I solemnly promised myself (and Herself) that we would never, ever, do anything like that again. And we haven't.

Wherever you go with a caravan, and whatever the weather, within minutes of arrival it is possible for you to have your feet up, warm and dry, with a pot of tea going and gentle music in the background: as the poet said, 'God's in His Heaven and all's right with the world'.

There are those who hate the sight of caravans – 'They clutter up the roads and befoul the countryside'. Some consider it distinctly 'non-U' – 'It's for gypsies. It's for people who wear brown shoes with blue suits, or can't afford "proper" holidays'. I confess to being guilty of entertaining many of these thoughts years ago, but we are now completely hooked and have been for years. It is a great hobby. As I said: more a way of life. So if you are teetering on the brink, gentle reader, and don't know the first thing about caravanning or where to start, then read on. I hope you will find this collection of jottings at least helpful.

CARRYING POWER A STEP FURTHER.

Now you have the power to go further with the handiest of handy sized portable generators.

Light, compact and ideal for caravanners, campers and everyone who needs a power source that's easy to carry.

Send for your Honda Generator brochure soon.

- - - - - - - - - - - - - -

To: Honda Advertising Services, Thames House, 5 Church Street, Twickenham, Middlesex TW1 3NJ. Please send me the Honda Handy Generator brochure, price list and name of my nearest dealer.

Name ....

Address ....

....

HONDA
DESIGNED BY PERFECTIONISTS

Chapter 1

Choosing a Caravan

General Guide to Selection

Caravans, like cars, boats, aircraft, cameras or hi-fi equipment, have progressed almost beyond recognition during the past few years, both in technical specification and aesthetic appeal, and of course prices have progressed accordingly. There are now about 400 new models to choose from. British caravans produced after 1970 will comply with the specifications laid down in British Standard No. 4626 which protects caravanners' interests in many areas including hygiene, safety etc.

Many of the provisions of BS 4626 are now already out of date and are under constant review. A new British Standard for caravans, BS 6765 was in the process of formulation, and it was intended to replace BS 4626 entirely. Parts 3 and 4 of BS 6765 are already effective, and these relate to low voltage (12 volt) electrics and to the construction of undergear, that is chassis, brakes, suspension, coupling head etc.

With the move towards standardisation within the EC, it now seems likely that BS 6765 will never see the light of day in its completed form. Instead, a new 'European Norm' is being drawn up by joint consultation between EC member countries, and parts 3 and 4 of BS 6765 which are already effective in the UK will form the basis for the new European Norm. In addition to the areas already covered by parts 3 and 4 of the old British Standard, there will be several other sections of caravan construction to be catered for. Gas installations, and the fitting of flame failure safety devices on cooker hobs is just one example.

It is unlikely that the proposed European Norm will be agreed and in place before 1995/96, in the meantime BS 6765, so far as it goes, will remain the yardstick for British caravan manufacturers and references to BS 6765 in this book must be taken in the context of its ultimate replacement by a joint European/British standard.

TOWBARS – OUT OF SIGHT – BUT NOT OUT OF MIND

For most of us a car is the single biggest investment after a house, closely followed by a caravan. Why then is the vital piece of equipment that connects the two, costing so little by comparison, giving so little thought, with holidays compromised and lives risked by trying to save a few pounds on a cheap, often sub-standard, untested towbar?

There are a host of companies, manufacturing towbars. Some garages may even offer to "knock you one up". This option should definitely be avoided, big and beefy does not necessarily mean safe and just what guarantees are you getting?

One of the best indications of safety is British Standard certification, so first make sure that the towing bracket you choose meets British Standard AU114b, or the equivalent international standard ISO 3853. To meet these standards the bracket must meet certain design and manufacturing criteria including height of the ball above the ground and clearances between ball and the rear of the vehicle. Much more important, the bracket design must be subjected to – and pass – a rigorous fatigue test consisting of two million cycles at loads calculated from the vehicle manufacturers' recommended towing weights and specifically designed to simulate the stresses and strains that a bracket would encounter during a lifetime of hard use.

Remember, look at the small print, does the manufacturer claim a complete 2 million stress test or is it only the height above ground that meets the BS standard.

Having checked a towbar passes all the BS tests the next important point to look at is attachment points. All car manufacturers take into account the possibility of the vehicle being used for towing and engineer the chassis/frame/body accordingly. Many will have fixing points already drilled or marked, unfortunately for a number of reasons these attachment points may not lead to the most economical way of manufacturing a towbar, as a result some towbar manufacturers may require special attachment points to be drilled. Be warned, by not using recognised attachment points you could be voiding at least part of the vehicle warranty and, if an incident were to occur you would be leaving yourself open to criticism. Anyway, if the vehicle designer has gone to the trouble of including proper mounting points isn't it common sense to use them?

Arguably the best all-round indicator of quality and safety is the Automobile Association's "Seal of Approval", only awarded to products meeting high standards of design and manufacture. For towbars to gain this coveted award the AA has, since 1986, insisted on the use of vehicle manufacturers' recommended mounting points, full compliance with BS and ISO standards and the inclusion with the towing bracket of a Data Plate stating maximum nose loads and towing weights amongst the critical criteria.

To a prospective towbar purchaser the AA seal of approval is undoubtedly the best indicator of highest quality design, test, manufacturing and attachment procedures.

York Towbars were first marketed around 20 years ago. In 1985 a testing rig was installed to help qualified engineers improve the quality of design and manufacture. Testing in accordance with BS AU114b York gained the AA seal of approval; currently the only towing bracket manufacturer to do so.

York's corporate position has safety and quality as the main priorities, this is backed by the company's accreditation to BS 5750 for design and manufacture. David Clements, general manager of York Towbars is proud that these high levels of quality have been possible without major impact on retail prices which remain competitive with lesser designs and adds: "If you have any queries concerning towbars the experienced York technical team is only too pleased to help. In the past this has even included manufacturing customised towbars".

York can be contacted on Tel 0547 528534 or 0547 520690 so, if you are in any doubt give them a ring, the price of a 'phone call is nothing compared with peace of mind.

1993 *Wisp 404*
Photos courtesy of Elddis Caravans Ltd.

1993 *Swift Corniche 15/2.*

1993 *Swift Diamond Corvette*
Photos courtesy of Swift Caravans Ltd.

1993 *Crusader Sirocco*

Examples of caravans available.

Fire-proof upholstery and smoke alarms have been catered for and regulations regarding their use are now in force. Reference to these is made in Chapter 5.

Purchasers of second-hand caravans less than 20 years old should ensure that they do in fact comply with BS 4626, as amended, and a National Caravan Council (NCC) Certificate badge on a caravan confirms that it does. There are however, many caravans about which are much older than this and are still giving good service.

Some of the hints and comments in this book will be applicable only to older caravans. Modern sophisticated fittings and systems make these comments irrelevant to more recent models.

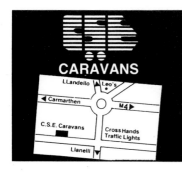
I hope that you will find advice and comment in this by no means comprehensive tome to help you with the sort of caravan you are considering.

Let us establish straight away, therefore, that you can acquire an older caravan, in habitable order, for a few hundred pounds, or you can part with well over £20,000 for an upmarket model complete with sophisticated trappings and comforts.

Somewhere in between is probably the van you want. Two things usually govern your choice – what you can afford, and what your car can comfortably tow.

The Towcar

What your car can comfortably tow is most important. There is an old adage that says you should have the smallest caravan you can comfortably live in, towed by the largest car you can afford. Although this is a bit extreme, you should try not to allow the actual laden weight (ALW) of your van to exceed 85 per cent of the kerbside weight of your car. (The ALW is the ex-works weight of your van plus all its contents. We will see in a later chapter how the contents rapidly add up to a formidable amount of weight.) Manufacturers will state a Maximum Laden Weight (MLW) for a van. This is the very maximum weight for which the caravan is designed for normal use when being towed on the road laden. The ALW should always be kept below the MLW. You could be outside the law if the MLW is exceeded. Although there is no specific regulation to this effect, the law might decide that 'the weight, distribution, packing and adjustment of the load' caused or might cause danger on a road. (Construction and Use Regulation 100.)

These expressions are fairly easy to understand. The Maximum Laden Weight, set by the caravan manufacturer, is the absolute limit of weight that the chassis and suspension can safely carry. The Actual Laden Weight is the total weight of the van after you have put all your gear in it, and of course this should never exceed the MLW, better that it should be less than the MLW by a safe margin. The 'payload' of the caravan is the difference between the ex-works weight ie a totally empty caravan, and the Maximum Laden Weight.

Now here I must try to avoid confusing you, but some new expressions are creeping in. A few chapters further on we see how we are living in an era of change, for example we are quoted weights and measurements in both metric and Imperial units. One day it will all be metric, but at present we have to cope with both. Now for some more new ideas.

We mentioned a couple of pages ago that the proposed European Norm will replace the British Standards to which caravans are now built. When this becomes effective, the well known phrases such as Maximum Laden Weight and 'payload' will be replaced by new and equally simple expressions, and they are as follows:

- Maximum Authorised Weight (MAW). This will replace the old term Max Laden Weight or Max Gross Weight, which were one and the same thing.

- Maximum Technical Permissible Weight (MTPW). Both this and MAW will be set by the manufacturer, and the MTPW will either be equal to or higher than the MAW. If higher, then the manufacturer is allowing an extra safety margin. It will be rather like the old Actual Laden Weight being kept below the Max Laden Weight.

- Finally, the Caravan Allowable Payload (CAP). This equates to what we presently call the 'payload' or 'loading margin', and it will obviously be the difference between the ex-works weight and the Max Authorised Weight.

These new terms are not yet current jargon in caravan circles, and don't appear in manufacturers' brochures. They will eventually however, as we move from British Standards towards European Norms. For simplicity therefore we will stick to the terms which most caravanners are familiar with, and throughout this book we will continue to refer to Max Laden Weight, Actual Laden Weight and so on. Sufficient unto the day . . .

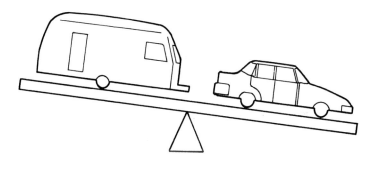

Laden weight

Weight and engine size

This van/car weight ratio is vital in arriving at a safe and manageable road outfit, but in addition to the weight of the car you must also consider its engine size and its resultant power and torque. A car which achieves maximum torque at lower engine revs is preferable, since towing involves lower speeds. In this respect diesel engines have a distinct advantage.

Most motor manufacturers make available the recommended towing weights for their models, and although some of these need to be taken with a pinch of salt, you should consider their recommendations when choosing your caravan.

It is not enough to be able to tow your caravan on a level road. You may have to start the outfit off from standstill on a gradient, preferably without burning out your clutch. How much power is needed?

A good rule of thumb is to have a car whose engine can produce a minimum of 40 brake horse power (BHP) per ton of outfit weight. That is total weight of car and caravan combined. This sounds a bit complicated but it is simple to calculate. Take a car, for example, whose kerb weight is 990 kgs and whose engine output is 85 BHP (see the car handbook), and add the actual laden weight of the caravan, say 840 kgs. In this case the caravan is about 84 per cent of the kerb weight of the car, which is acceptable.

Now add the weight of two passengers plus their luggage, say 160 kgs. Now we have a total outfit weight of 990 + 840 + 160 = 1990 kgs. On the basis of 1015 kgs equals 1 ton, we have an outfit weight of 1.96 tons. To get 40 BHP per ton, therefore, the car must produce 1.96 × 40, which is 78.4 BHP, and this is covered by the car's 85 BHP. In this example we are taking a typical modern 13 foot van and an average family car.

A good towcar will ideally have a fairly close-ratio gearbox ie. not too wide a gap between gears, particularly between 4th and 5th.

A classic towcar for some years has been the Citroen BX 19 Diesel. As a diesel it is very economical and it could have been made even more so with a slightly higher 5th gear, which the car could easily handle as a solo vehicle. However, it would not have won the coveted 'Towcar of the Year' as often as it has with a higher 5th gear.

With upwards of ¾ ton caravan on tow, little use could have been made of a higher 5th gear, whereas with its present excellent gearbox it will sail up many a hill in 5th where a towcar with a 'longer' 5th gear will have to change down.

Engine power and gear ratios could take up a chapter by themselves, but this is not intended as a technical thesis. It is sufficient to say that the most economical solo cars are by no means the most economical towcars. You must have sufficient power from your engine, to have a little in reserve when towing.

To arrive quickly at the likely ALW of the caravan, subtract the ex-works weight from the MLW (see the caravan hand-book). This figure gives the van's 'payload'. Since this is the absolute maximum permissible, you should aim at about three-quarters of the 'book' payload as the amount of gear you will load in the caravan.

In the past some caravans were advertised as having artificially low MLWs. This appeared to make them towable by fairly small cars, but this was only achieved by leaving a very small allowance for loading luggage and accessories, ie 'payload'. BS 4626 put a stop to this and defines the payload allowance as follows: it must be a minimum of 15 per cent of MLW *plus* an allowance of 15 kgs for gas cylinders, plus another 15 kgs if no heater is fitted, plus another 30 kgs if there is no refrigerator.

Since some of your weights are metric and some imperial, the following guide might be helpful for your calculations:

10 kgs equals 22 lbs.
10 lbs equals 4.54 kgs.

All this talk of caravan/car weights sounds off-putting but it is simple in principle and quite vital to the stability, safety and sometimes the legality of your outfit. You must never exceed the recommended MLW (or MGW) of your caravan, and never allow the ALW (Actual Laden Weight) to exceed the kerb weight of your car. Ideally, the caravan/car towing ratio should be 85 per cent maximum.

Checklist: Matching caravan to car

● What is the Maximum Laden Weight (or Maximum Gross Weight or Maximum Design Weight) of your proposed caravan?

● What is its weight empty (ex-works weight)? Remember that the figure stated by the manufacturer may vary by ± 5 per cent in practice. Check your actual figure on a public weighbridge.

● Subtract 2 from 1 to calculate the payload available. Is this adequate? (See page 77 for weights of essential extra equipment.)

● What is the *kerbside weight* of your car? Is the *laden* weight of the van less than this – preferably no more than 85 per cent?

● Does your car engine produce *at least* 40 BHP for every ton of 'outfit weight'? (This is the *combined* weight of *loaded* caravan and *loaded* car.)

If you cannot answer 'yes' to 3, 4 and 5 you are looking at the wrong caravan, or need a larger car.

Accommodation and Size

Having decided on the weight of caravan your car can tow, you can now narrow things down a little by considering how many people it must sleep.

Four-to five-berth vans are commonplace and may be in the 12 foot to 15 foot body length group. Six-berth vans tend to be from 14 foot to 16 foot or even up to 20 feet, although there are many ingenious designs which incorporate children's or larger beds which fold away out of sight in the daytime, producing surprisingly generous sleeping facilities at night in quite modestly sized caravans. (These arrangements, however, can often be at the expense of sufficient space to

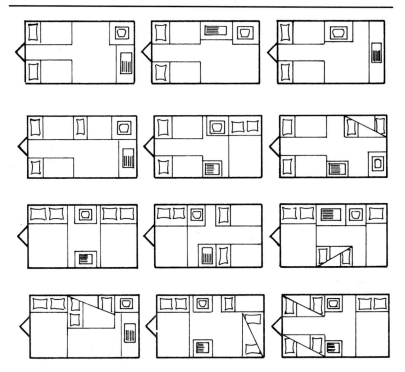

Some examples of internal layouts

operate freely in the kitchen area, or they may hinder opening the toilet door fully.) It is important also to check that, when children are in bed, there is absolutely unrestricted access to the caravan door, at all times, in the event of fire.

Sleeping, cooking and dining

Caravans with more than two berths usually provide a double bed in the front sitting/dining area (these beds can be a bit on the small side, often no more than 3 feet 10 inches to 4 feet wide), plus perhaps another double bed at the rear of the caravan or a number of single bunks, often one above the other. These multi-berth layouts usually place the kitchen area on one side of the caravan – amidships – whereas a two-berth caravan has a double bonus. The arrangement is usually one bed of at least 6 feet × 6 feet 6 inches or two roomy singles, and the kitchen is along the rear wall of the caravan. This is

31

known as an 'end kitchen' and is roomier than the side-wall variety. It is made possible by the absence of beds, bunks etc at the rear end. The cupboards and toilet compartment are also correspondingly roomier in a two-berth caravan.

Alternatively, a roomy two berth can feature the large double bed at the front end, have the kitchen along a side wall, leaving scope for a spacious shower/toilet/dressing room, complete with wardrobe, across the entire width of the caravan at the rear end.

Type and positioning of toilet

Mention of the toilet compartment is important. Although sanitation is discussed fully in Chapter 7, it is worth reminding you now to consider whether you will have a portable (chemical) toilet or not. Perhaps you will only use established sites with permanent toilet facilities. If your caravan has a chemical toilet, will it go outside in a special toilet tent, or inside the caravan in the loo compartment? If the latter, is the compartment large enough to stand the toilet on the floor with sufficient room to allow you to stand at the wash basin? Loos in more modern caravans tend to be more generously designed, often with a built-in shower and a built-in chemical toilet (see also Chapter 7).

Awning

Finally, on the subject of how many beds you want, think about an awning. An awning is a weatherproof type of tent, joined simply and firmly to the side of the van. It has a framework of light-weight poles, and can effectively more than double the living space of your caravan. A brood of children therefore need not bar you from caravanning, or commit you to an over-large caravan. When our four children were small, we slept at least two of them on comfortable camp beds in the awning and also used it for storing folding chairs and table, tinned food, beach mats, wellies and all the other junk a family on holiday collects. More about awnings in Chapter 4.

Checklist: Accommodation

● Two-person families need a two-berth caravan, which is no problem.

● For larger families, could you sleep the children in a caravan awning, or even in a separate tent? Given this solution, does the caravan enable you all to eat together?

● Is the layout convenient for your needs?

● Are the beds adequate for extra tall or wide crew members?

● Is there sufficient wardrobe/locker space for all the clobber for larger crews?

● Could you be 'at home' in the caravan? Does it feel right?

Mini and Folding Caravans

When considering the sort of caravan to buy, don't overlook a folding van. Folders, as they are called, are cleverly designed so that the side and end walls are hinged about half way up; all four fold inwards, and the flat roof settles down on top. You then have a flat-topped trailer about three feet high, well below the height of your car. Better rear vision and much more economical towing plus greater stability are usually the result.

Folders have ingenious hinged cupboards and fittings that assemble quickly and easily into place, but often suffer from fewer high-level lockers and shelves. They may be heavier and more expensive that 'budget' rigid caravans but are often easier to store. When compared with the frontal area of 50 odd square feet of a rigid caravan, their fuel economy and general ease of towing are undisputed.

Folders vary from models which fold right down on to a flat trailer to semi-rigid versions with a pop-up roof section for added headroom. They vary in size from two-to four-berth and also vary considerably in weight. The four-berth 'Casita

The Carousel 10/2 T, showing erection procedure.
Photo courtesy of Gobur Caravans Ltd.

Lion' has a Maximum Laden Weight of about 15.5 cwt, whereas the two-berth 'Fleurette' weighs in at 11.5 cwt. This is a very
realistic towing proposition for a couple with, say, a Vauxhall
Nova or a Fiesta or Metro.

The Gloucestershire based firm Eriba produces a large range
of compact vans with pop-up tops. The smallest of these is a
triumph of ingenuity in design. With a body length of 10 feet,
and a width of 5 feet one inch, the 'Puck' weighs in at just 8
cwt, but only has a maximum laden weight of 10 cwt, so the
margin for loading is small. A van like this can be towed
comfortably by a small hatchback, and presents few problems
when it comes to winter stowage.

Gobur Caravans of Melton Constable, Norfolk manufacture a
range of compact folding caravans, including the 'Slimline'
which is only 5 feet 8 inches wide. Their range of folders are
sturdily built and well equipped. The company trade direct
with the public and also carry a stock of secondhand Gobur trade-
ins, all of which are factory checked (see Useful Addresses).

It is worth noting, however, that 'small' and 'compact' do
not necessarily mean cheap. There are conventional rigid
caravans available (albeit with modest specifications) which
can financially undercut many folders.

Checklist: Mini vans and folders

- If you are going to tow with a car with a 1300cc engine or smaller, you need a mini van.

- Weigh up the advantages of a 'folder' (much more economical towing, perhaps better rear vision, easier storage) against the disadvantages (possibly more expensive, and more limited specification). Also, there is a more limited carrying capacity on the move.

- *Remember.* Apply the guidelines given in the checklist following the 'Payload' section (see page 77), with regard to relative weights of caravan and car. The same applies to engine power related to caravan weight. These guidelines apply to mini and folding vans just as much as to conventional caravans.

Caravan Construction

You know the maximum weight of the caravan you want and you know how many it must sleep. The next major consideration is price, and your budget will affect the age of the van you buy. Will it be new? Two years old? Seven years? Twelve years? It is worth noting here just how much caravans have changed and improved in recent years.

Chassis

The most noticeable advance has been in the area of weight saving. A modern caravan can therefore be larger than its same weight counterpart of nine or ten years ago. Lightweight galvanized or alloy chassis are now used in conjunction with a completely new van body construction. Instead of a number of heavy transverse wooden joists topped by a timber floor, as in house construction, caravan floors now consist of a bonded plywood and styrene sandwich which is lighter and stronger. Also the walls and roof are of sandwich construction and are lined with polystyrene, a material light in weight, but affording considerable

improvement in thermal insulation and resistance to conden-
sation. Very few caravans are now made on the old style heavy
wooden framework.

Windows

During the late seventies the use of glass windows disappeared. There was government legislation in the pipeline to
make all caravan glass windows in toughened glass, as in cars.
This would have added to both cost and weight, and
manufacturers reacted quickly to produce light-weight acrylic
windows, usually in the form of a double skin with the outer
skin tinted. Double glazing therefore is now almost a standard
feature, and as metal frames are unnecessary more weight is
saved. Exterior windows of caravans manufactured after
November 1977 must be constructed either of safety glass or
of safety glazing. Safety glass must be to BS 857 or 5282: safety
glazing is not covered by a BS but means material other than
glass, such as acrylic, which if fractured does not fly into
fragments.

Internal fixtures

In addition to basic construction innovation, internal
equipment and appointments have continued to advance.
New, up-market caravans feature hot water systems, often
with a roomy built-in shower with electric water pumps.
Internal warmth in modern caravans can be provided by
thermostatically controlled hot air or hot water central heating
systems run by gas heaters with external flues. A much
simpler gas stove with no flue can provide an adequate
alternative, and can be fitted inexpensively to an older
caravan. Adequate ventilation is absolutely essential, however,
when using a gas appliance without an external flue. The
subject of ventilation is discussed further in Chapter 13.

Probably the fastest growing innovation has been 'plumbed
in' mains electricity. Few new caravans are now without it.
(See also Chapter 9 on mains electricity.)

Additions and modifications

On the basis that today's extra luxuries are tomorrow's standard fittings, your older, second-hand caravan may well be without heating, electric water pump, hot water system, fridge or oven. All these can be supplied and fitted – at a price – by a good caravan dealer, and much of the work can be installed by a competent DIY man. If you are going to install gas appliances yourself, however, do have your finished system pressure-checked at a dealer's workshop, to ensure that it is absolutely free of leaks. If you install electrical mains you are strongly advised to have such installations inspected and certified by a contractor approved by the NICEIC, that is the National Inspection Council for Electrical Installation Contracting. (See Chapter 9 on mains electrics.)

Remember that all these extras constitute additional weight. Watch your recommended MLW. In this connection, two heavy items are the fridge and the oven. If you can afford only one of these, because of either cost or weight, go for the fridge every time. Even an average English summer will see your milk, meat, butter etc 'going off' in no time, and for continental summer holidays a fridge is a must. To us, an oven is very low priority – Herself feeds us very well indeed with gas rings and a grill. (We will come back to this in the section on catering in Chapter 12.)

You can go on adding extras indefinitely. For example, I have installed a car radio/cassette player and two speakers in our van – a standard feature in new luxury vans.

To sum up, then, the less you pay for your van the greater will be its probable age and weight, and the fewer modern amenities it will have. If you have a fixed amount to spend, bear in mind that to remain within your budget it may be better to buy a good quality, well-appointed caravan that is three or four years old and has been well maintained, than to buy a brand new caravan from the lower end of the price range, with a more basic specification. With a family, it is also more sensible to buy a medium-size van and a good awning, than a large van to sleep everybody. The larger caravan will be more expensive, heavier and less manageable, and will need a larger car to tow it.

Second-hand caravans

Even if you are buying second-hand go to a reputable caravan dealer, who can give you sound advice and a guarantee on a not-too-old caravan, depending on price. Do take an experienced caravanner along with you if possible and take his or her advice.

Before selling a second-hand caravan a dealer must thoroughly check it on all points where safety is involved. If it proves faulty the dealer is liable. No such redress is available with a private sale.

Before the advent of polystyrene sandwich construction, caravans were built on a timber framework, and thousands of them are still in use. Moisture can eat into this framework, so it is essential carefully to check corners and seams in the metal outer cladding of the caravan and around window frames. Look for dried-out, flaking mastic filler. Check for damp-stains throughout the interior. Carefully and thoroughly inspect the entire chassis and corner steadies for rust. The same applies to brake linkages. Does the handbrake hold the caravan on a slope? Check for damp stains around water and waste-pipe joints. Check front and rear light clusters for damp. Get the dealer to plug the electrics into a test board, and check that all lights are working. Ask him to do a gas pressure test if this has not already been done. Gas leaks are dangerous, but easily checked on. Check the tyres less for tread wear than splits in the grooves, and tyre walls for cuts, splits, or bulges. Are they a matching pair for type and size? Check the chassis number – this is usually found on a metal plate fixed to the drawbar or die-stamped on to the frame. Plates with false numbers are too easily switched. A phone call to the chassis manufacturer or caravan dealer will confirm the age of the van. In case of difficulty in tracing the manufacturer contact the Caravan Club, or the National Caravan Council (see Useful Addresses). Take the caravan for a trial tow before you buy. Does it ride level (viewed from the end)? How are the brakes? Does it handle well and feel right?

Sadly, caravan thefts are increasing dramatically, and this is discussed in Chapter 14 which deals with security. The point is, don't feel hesitant about asking the history of a caravan you propose to buy. If you are offered a secondhand van at a suspiciously low price or you have doubts about its origins, note the chassis number and model, then make a phone call to either the Caravan Club or the National Caravan Council. Both bodies keep a computerised record of all stolen caravans.

If you have the misfortune to buy a caravan which subsequently proves to be stolen, then you are the loser. It legally belongs to the person from whom it was stolen, and your purchase money goes down the drain. Your only redress is from the one who stole it, and assuming you can find him, suing him is unlikely to bear fruit. Alternatively, if the dealer or person you bought it from is proved to have knowingly received stolen goods then you have a claim against him, but it is a costly, tedious and unpleasant business, so do be warned. There are a lot of stolen caravans about, and many are offered for resale.

Finally, before spending your last cent on a caravan, consider the extras it may need. If your caravan is second-hand some of these items may be included, and the dealer could well supply some items second-hand. You will certainly need two gas cylinders, plus a regulator valve and fresh and waste water containers. A fire extinguisher plus a fire blanket are strongly recommended, as are a 12-volt battery and battery box, and a chemical toilet. A water trolley makes life easier (a five-gallon container of water weighs 50 lbs!). A spare wheel plus jack and wheelbrace are essentials, and finally, perhaps on lower priority, come a fridge and suitable awning. (See also Chapter 4.)

Checklist: Caravan construction

● The older the caravan you are considering, the heavier it is likely to be (and the more likely to leak).

● Check seams and corners of body for damp.

● Check chassis and drawbar for anything more than superficial rust, and for structural weakness.

● Check corner steadies (the wind-down legs).

● Check brakes (including handbrake) and tyres.

● Check water and gas leaks.

● Check electrics.

● Check manufacturer's name and chassis number.

● Unless you are buying an old, low-priced caravan buy from a reputable dealer.

● If you are not confident that you know what you're about – take along someone who does. It could save·you a lot of regret.

● Tow it before you buy it, if possible.

Survey of Second-hand Caravans

Professional inspection

To end this chapter on choosing a caravan let me acquaint you with a service that is of great value to any buyer of a second-hand caravan.

Two organisations have recently implemented ideas similar to each other, that is, professional detailed inspection of caravans, similar to the inspection of second-hand cars as offered by the motoring organisations.

First, the RAC in conjunction with the Camping and Caravanning Club set up a scheme called Carascan. Soon after, Caracheck was launched by the Caravan Club in conjunction with National Breakdown (National Breakdown operate the Caravan Club's recovery scheme).

Both schemes offer a similar service which includes a detailed inspection of the interior and exterior (the bodywork) of the caravan, including a check on damp. Electrics, 12-volt and mains, gas system, wheels, tyres and suspension, chassis and towing gear, jockey wheel, corner steadies etc, all are thoroughly inspected. A report is submitted, with recommendations on any necessary work.

Costs charged by both organisations are similar and vary between about £60 and £80, depending on whether or not mains electrics are involved and whether you are actually a member of the relevant organisation. You don't need to be a member, however, to have a check carried out on a caravan.

These services are not cheap, but are well worth the outlay. If you are a newcomer to the game, you could save yourself the inspection fee many times over.

Carascan – details are available from your local RAC office or ring Carascan direct on 0203 694995.

Caracheck – details can be obtained from National Breakdown on 0532 393666, or from the Caravan Club on 0342 326944. (See Useful Addresses).

Chapter 2

Towing on the Road

Introduction

Towing is not difficult, although to begin with you are very conscious of this enormous white *thing* that fills your rear view mirror.

Towing Mirrors

Since many caravans do not afford through-vision via the front and back windows you rely on your side mirrors, and several makes of special clip-on towing mirrors are available. These project further out from the car than conventional side mirrors, which must not project more than 20 cms (8 inches). They enable you to see down the sides of your caravan and to the rear. Fitted on the off side of your car, one of these is really a must, and one on the near side is certainly advisable. Some continental countries require such a towing mirror – fitted on the left when towing – by law. In the UK, if you do not have through-vision via your internal mirror, two standard external mirrors is the minimum legal requirement.

Van size and speed

The caravan faithfully follows the path of the towing vehicle, and with properly adjusted brakes both will stop as quickly as a solo car. You must become familiar with the extra width behind you, and allow for it when overtaking or meeting other traffic. Some caravans are taller than others – be aware of your extra height at such places as filling stations with low canopies, footbridges etc.

On some roll-on roll-off ferries, not all caravans will fit underneath the mezzanine car decks at the sides of the main vehicle deck. Slightly taller caravans and those with certain rooftop TV aerials need to be loaded in the centre of the main vehicle deck, with the coaches and lorries. The shortfall in

headroom may only be a few inches or so, but enough to do a fair amount of damage.

I once had to conduct a heated exchange – in French – with a crew member who wanted to put my outfit underneath a mezzanine deck when I knew it would not actually fit. Fortunately the Entente Cordiale and common sense triumphed in the end.

When towing a caravan you are restricted to a speed of 50mph in the UK (60mph maximum on dual carriageways and motorways). It is no longer necessary to carry '50' stickers on the rear of the caravan or to display the respective weights on the caravan and car. You are urged, however, not to allow the *total* weight of the caravan to exceed 85 per cent of the weight of the car. Beyond this you could begin to sacrifice stability of the whole outfit.

When towing you may not use the right hand or outside lane of a motorway which has more than two lanes, unless an extra wide load takes up more than one lane.

On a narrow or winding road, do avoid holding up other

traffic. On such a road, with a queue of traffic behind you, pull into the side at the first opportunity and let the queue pass you.

When you first set off, keep your speed down until you become accustomed to the feel of the outfit. As a general rule, however, don't drive more slowly than necessary, although you must consider your permitted maximum speed and the principles of general road safety.

Your outfit will be 30 feet long or more, and not easy to overtake quickly. Don't bunch up with traffic in front of you. Leave ample room for larger and faster vehicles to overtake and pull in safely in front of you.

Pairs of caravan outfits in convoy are often guilty of this bad driving fault. If you are holidaying with friends and taking two vans, arrange to meet at your destination. You will find this much easier than playing 'follow my leader' and you will certainly cause less danger and aggravation to other road users.

If you must move in pairs *don't* sit on your buddy's tail. At 50 mph your stopping distance is 175 feet, *not* 20 feet. (Look it up in the new *Highway Code.*) When towing, add a little more for safety. True, an emergency stop with a caravan is perfectly feasible, but not really desirable. You don't really want all your cupboard doors to burst open at once.

Two caravan outfits driven close together occupy 80 feet of road or more – difficult for a large lorry to overtake in one bite and on a single carriageway road, almost impossible. Stay well back and leave ample space between the two outfits so that other vehicles can 'leapfrog' past you in safety.

After missed-altogether and incorrect signals, the next most common serious driving fault must surely be driving too close to the vehicle in front, and is even more hazardous when practised by two caravans in tandem. It's a lunatic philosophy under any circumstances; you don't get to your destination any quicker by tail-gateing the vehicle in front.

Caravanners, sadly, are often not the 'flavour of the month' with other road users. This is the result of thoughtless and selfish driving on the part of a few.

Overtaking

If you overtake a slower moving lorry, you may notice in your nearside mirror that the driver flashes the headlights when you have passed. This is to tell you that the rear of your caravan is now clear of the front of the lorry, so you can safely return to your nearside lane. The polite reply is to briefly flash your tail lights as a 'thank you' signal, and *keep moving*. Having passed the lorry, don't slow down and get in its way.

These headlight signals are not to be found in the *Highway Code* but they are widely practised by drivers of large goods vehicles, and I firmly believe in extending the same courtesy to the driver of a long LGV who overtakes your outfit. Almost invariably you will receive your 'thank you' in response.

If you are overtaken at some speed by a particularly large lorry or coach, you are often sucked sideways for an instant and your outfit swings to the right towards the overtaking vehicle. This happens particularly if it is passing you without leaving much room between that vehicle and yours. Don't over-react, don't brake suddenly. Keep a firm hold on your steering wheel and try to ease slightly over to your left. Don't wrench suddenly at your steering wheel, as this will only set up a 'snaking' reaction. It is an unpleasant sensation, but the situation rights itself within a couple of seconds or so. The main thing is not to be taken by surprise. Constantly use your offside mirror, particularly on motorways, and if you see a large vehicle moving up to overtake, ease into the left to increase the gap between the two outfits.

Snaking occurs when the caravan starts to wag from side to side, eventually wagging the car also. This should rarely occur with an outfit that is not overloaded or badly balanced. If snaking does occur, however, do *not* brake or accelerate. Lift your foot off the accelerator, let the speed fall away, and stability should soon be restored.

Stabilizers

Mention of snaking leads on to the subject of stabilizers. These are a tensioning device usually fitted between the

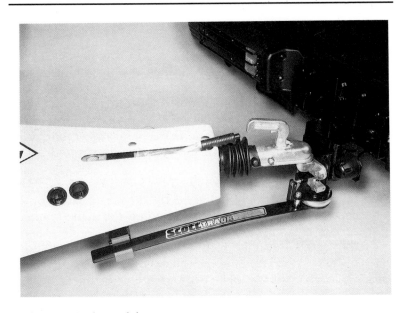

The Scott TRA/QR stabilizer.
Photo courtesy of Scott Halleys.

towbar of your car and the drawbar of the caravan. There are several on the market, all good. I use and recommend the 'Scott'. This type incorporates a strong leaf spring which tends to counteract the tendency of the nose-weight of the caravan to depress the rear of the car. It also exerts a resistance to the turning movement between caravan and car. While this is not strong enough to prevent the caravan being towed round a corner, it very effectively resists any tendency of the van to wag from side to side. At the time of writing the 'Scott' stabilizer costs about £50–£60. It is easy to fit, simple to attach and detach, and is money very wisely spent. In addition to stabilizers which use the friction damper principle, one or two new models are available where the stabilizer is fixed rigidly to the drawbar or coupling head, and actually grips the car towball very tightly. In these cases the towball is dry rather than greased, and the jaws of the stabilizer have a 'Teflon' or similar coating. Two well tried examples of this type are the Westphalia SSK and the Al Ko AKS 2000. Though more expensive than a conventional stabilizer these 'grip the towball' devices are both simple to·operate and very effective.

Checklist: Towing

- Equip your car with towing mirrors.

- The speed limit for towing a caravan is 50mph on single carriageways, and 60mph on dual carriageways, including motorways.

- *Don't* hold up other, faster traffic.

- Keep a sensible distance from the vehicle in front, and leave room for others to overtake you.

- Do fit a stabilizer.

- Remember: good driving, whether towing or not, consists mostly of *good manners* and *common sense*.

- On motorways keep a good lookout behind for 'heavies'.

When I see caravans on main roads swaying from side to side, I am surprised that more caravanners do not appreciate the value of a good quality stabilizer.

Loading – Weight Distribution

Weight distribution is vital in obtaining a stable caravan. A van must be nose-heavy if it is to give a stable, safe, snake-free tow. Aim for about 100lbs nose-weight or a little more, ie approximately 7 per cent of the ALW. Some caravans have an above-average noseweight. Check your car manufacturer's maximum recommended trailer noseweight.

You can buy a simple spring balance with a graduated scale which sits on the ground and you lower the coupling head of the caravan on to it to get a reading. Simpler still, use your bathroom scales. Don't stand the jockey wheel on the scales – you won't get a correct reading. Use a short piece of wood directly under the coupling head, making sure the caravan is level.

Gas cylinders carried on the drawbar of the caravan, usually in a locker, will contribute towards nose-weight. In a rear-end

Weigh-It nose weight gauge.
Photo courtesy of W4 Ltd.

kitchen van, the fridge and/or oven will tend to offset this. You must experiment with your loading until experience tells you how to distribute your gear. Heavy items such as awnings, awning poles, boxes of food (and crates of brown ale) should go on the caravan floor near the centre, ie over the axle. Keep most of the weight on the floor or in lockers under the beds. Avoid weight at the rear end of the caravan, which contributes to a tendency to swing from side to side. Don't load up the eye-level cupboards and lockers with heavy items – you want as low a centre of gravity on the loaded caravan as possible. Don't just cram it all in and set off with an overloaded, badly distributed van-full. Plan carefully. Only recently, on a delightful wooded site in the Vendee region of France, we sat, glass in hand, and watched with growing disbelief as a French couple prepared their caravan for departure. Our interest was first aroused by the spectacle of Madame going carefully over the outside of the awning with a pink feather duster, which drew an unprintable comment from Herself. The awning was then collapsed and stowed, with bursts of advice from the contestants in the ongoing game of boules, which seemed to be held all day, every day, on a nearby vacant pitch.

With all surplus gear stowed, Monsieur reversed his car to

the van and finally wound up his corner steadies. As he raised the last rear steady, the nose of the caravan reared up like some primeval dinosaur, and the van settled on its tail at an angle of 45 degrees to the ground. It was unbelievable.

'Oh la la!' cried Madame. Boules was abandoned, the players swarming round the van, some bearing down on the drawbar, others lifting at the rear.

I dearly wanted a photograph of this spectacle, but of course the camera was in the car, the car was locked and the keys were God knows where.

Meanwhile, with much straining, the coupling head of the caravan was forced down onto the car's towball and latched. The rear of the Renault rose a perceivable two or three inches. The whole operation was volubly directed by the chef de boules, an impressively stout gent in trousers, flip-flops, vest and beret, a Gauloise seemingly glued to the lower lip.

The van sagged visibly at the back. Heaven knows what was loaded into it, but no attempt was made to move it. Electrics were attached, also – give him his due – a stabilizer. Everyone stood back with murmurs of satisfaction. Monsieur and she of the pink feather duster shook hands all round, to

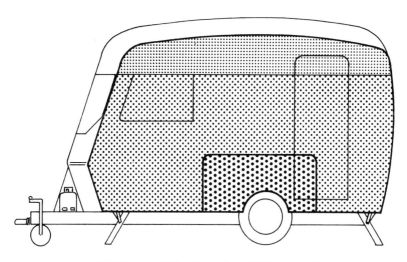

light load medium load heavy load

Load distribution

49

cries of 'à l'annee prochaine' and 'bon route', climbed aboard and moved off. Boules was resumed.

We ourselves left a couple of days later, bound for Southern Brittany. We scanned the roadside in vain near the campsite for signs of a totally decimated, tail-heavy French caravan. How the outfit handled on tow one can only imagine. I do know it was the most dangerous piece of caravanning malpractice I think I have ever seen. I do wish I had taken a photograph.

Checklist: Loading

- Find the best nose-weight for your outfit – somewhere between 100 and 150lbs perhaps. Check it every time you load up. Don't guess.

- Keep weighty items down at floor level and amidships (over the axle).

- Wedge loose items firmly in place.

- The centre of gravity must be kept low.

- If you don't need it, don't take it!.

Tyres

If you buy an older caravan fitted with cross-ply tyres, they are certainly past their useful life. The safe lifespan of a caravan tyre is about five years, regardless of treadwear. So buy new radials anyway.

Tyre pressure

Before starting a journey, always check your tyre pressures on caravan and car. Your caravan handbook will give recommended pressures. If in doubt, your caravan dealer will advise you. If the caravan nose-weight is on the high side or if your car is heavily laden, it is perhaps worth increasing the normal pressure in your car's rear tyres by 2 or 3lbs psi, but check your car handbook for advice on tyre pressures when towing or carrying heavy loads. Do not over-inflate tyres, however, for normal running as this will result in increased tyre wear and decreased grip. Remember always to check the pressures with *cold* tyres, not after a run. *Never* mix cross-ply and radials on the van. Also regularly check that the wheel nuts are tightened to the setting specified by the caravan manufacturer, using a torque wrench.

A torque wrench is a large wrench or spanner which will accept different sized sockets, and is adjustable so that a nut may be screwed up to exactly the correct tightness – no more. Over-tightening wheel nuts can be just as dangerous as having them too loose. A torque wrench can be bought at most car accessory dealers. (See Chapter 13 (Wheel Nuts) for details of actual torque settings.)

Hitching Up

Hooking your loaded caravan on to the car is probably the next task. Probably you can manfully pick up this 100–150lbs of nose-weight and, with the family pushing the loaded caravan, you can all struggle towards the car, but better still bring the mountain to Mahomet. The family will not thank you for acquiring a pre-holiday hernia, so leave the caravan where it is – on level ground if possible. Raise up the coupling head at the front of the caravan by winding the jockey wheel stem until the coupling is two or three inches above the height of the towball on the car.

Ask someone to stand by the coupling on the caravan with a hand held up directly over the coupling and high enough to be seen through the rear window of the car. Slowly reverse the car up to the caravan, aiming to position the towball on the car close to the caravan coupling, a few inches to either side of it. This is easy to say, not always easy to do. A good tip is to fix a small piece of white adhesive paper to the inside of the car rear window, dead central from the side to side aspect, right over the towball. Height is not critical – about halfway up the window will do.

You need a similar patch on the inside front caravan window, again dead central. Lining up these two marks in

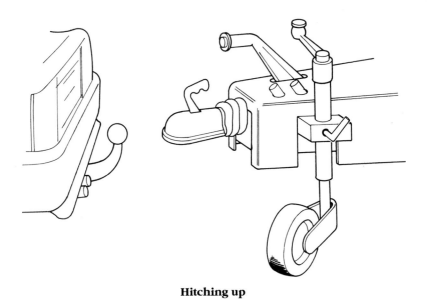

Hitching up

your car rear view mirror, as you reverse up to the van, enables you easily to position the towball and coupling head within a few inches of each other. Expect a burst of applause from onlookers. If the car can be stopped with towball and coupling level with each other, and a few inches to one side of each other, it is a simple matter to swing the front end of the caravan to whichever side is necessary in order to position the coupling directly over the towball on the car. In this position, simply wind down the jockey wheel stem until the caravan coupling locks over the towball. Ensure that the coupling is fully engaged over the towball and locked.

Note that you cannot swing the front of the caravan to either side unless the van handbrake is in 'Off' position – or disengaged; hence the desirability of hooking up on level ground. Now reverse-wind the jockey wheel, see the caravan coupling lift the back of the car. This ensures that the coupling is fully locked on to the ball.

Next, wind the jockey wheel back into its tube, or housing, then unclamp the tube and pull it up as far as it will go, until the jockey wheel itself is located tight up underneath the draw bar, and re-clamp it securely. The wheel is now well clear of the road for towing.

With the caravan hooked on to the car, fasten the safety chain or wire, which is attached to the van handbrake, round the car's towbar if possible, not the towball neck. This safety chain ensures that in the unlikely event of the caravan becoming detached from the car, or the car towball breaking, the caravan's handbrake will be applied just prior to the safety chain breaking as the car continues on its way.

Next attach your stabilizer, if fitted, to car and caravan, and finally plug in your electric leads from the van into the 7-pin sockets on the car. Modern outfits *must* have two such leads, plugs and sockets, due to the necessity to cater for high intensity fog lights on the caravan if it is to be towed by a car fitted with rear fog lights.

Having plugged in, get your tireless crew to stand behind the caravan and check all the rear lights as you operate them in the car. Left and right indicators, stop lights, rear and number plate lights, fog lights if fitted and, finally, the forward facing caravan side lights. Remember also to check your hazard lights.

Number one son, himself a recent convert to caravanning, actually managed to plug the 12N plug into the car socket *upside down*. Plug and socket have a projection and groove which renders this error virtually impossible, but he managed it.

The mistake was discovered when another caravanner, whom he had overtaken earlier, caught him up at a service station and advised him that when he moved to the left his right indicator showed, and when moving right the left one showed. Chris assured the bewildered fellow traveller that this was far from normal, and discovered the upside down plug. So be warned.

This, incidentally, highlights the need for checking all lights before setting off. Your crew should call out 'left' and 'right' as indicators are tested, not just 'OK'.

On caravans manufactured after October 1990, you will find an extra set of road lights known as 'outline marker lights'. These are now a European Community/British Government requirement. They are found high up on the sides of a caravan, midway along its length, and show a white light to the front and a red light to the rear, similar to the lights found on the sides of a large lorry.

Before moving off, check that the caravan jockey wheel is fully raised up and clamped firmly, the van handbrake is off, the manual reversing catch (on older vans) is released, and the caravan door closed and locked. Before finally closing the van door you should have checked that all windows are shut and fastened, the roof light closed, all cupboard and locker doors fastened, and no loose items left to bang about inside the caravan. Ensure that gas cylinders, whether carried in caravan or car, are securely located and in an upright position.

You now have a loaded caravan hooked on to a loaded car. Take a critical look from the side at the attitude of caravan and car. If the van appears nose-down, and the car sits there tail-down and nose-up, then you either have too great a nose-weight on the van or inadequate rear suspension on your car. Riding with car and caravan tilted like this you will severely dazzle oncoming drivers at night, even with dipped headlights, and you will not get the smoothest and safest ride. Some cars (eg Citroen) have self-levelling suspension systems which automatically compensate for the effect of caravan nose-weight. There are, however, many simple gadgets on the market to assist or 'beef up' a car's rear suspension, depending on the type of suspension your car has, ie leaf springs, trailing arms, coil springs etc. Special shock absorbers, coil springs containing inflated rubber balls and other devices are available, and many are advertised in caravanning magazines. Again, your caravan dealer will give ready advice on how to deal with the problem of a tail-down towcar.

Two of our earlier cars had coil springs on the rear suspension, and in each case I bought a pair of extra springs to fit inside the existing coils, and these effectively stiffened up the rear suspension to cope easily with the nose weight of the caravan. A simple DIY job.

Checklist: Hitching up

- Is coupling of caravan *securely* locked over towball on car? (*Most important!*)

- Jockey wheel fully raised and firmly clamped?

- Handbrake of caravan fully off?

- Safety chain secured to car?

- Manual reversing catch (old vans only) off?

- Electric plug(s) connected to car socket(s)?

- Check that all lights on caravan are working – particularly indicators.

- Are all caravan cupboard doors shut and fastened?

- Roof light(s) closed?

- Caravan door locked? Keys in your pocket and not still in the van door?

- Of course you had both car and caravan serviced, tyre pressures checked etc, before setting off.

Unhitching and Levelling

Now, after loading and joining caravan and car, and driving carefully and sensibly, you and your crew arrive at your chosen site. In Chapter 11 we will talk about the different types of caravan site, both at home and abroad.

Let's say you have arrived at a farmer's field. The spot you choose should be as level as possible. Avoid going to the bottom of a slope, since if it rains heavily the ground may become waterlogged, making it virtually impossible to push the caravan back up again on leaving. Towing, except with a four-wheel drive vehicle, would be out of the question because of wheel-spin.

Detaching caravan from car is the reverse process of hitching up. Having found your level site, apply the hand-brake of the van, detach the electric lead or leads between caravan and car, and remove the stabilizer and brake safety chain. Release the clamp holding the jockey wheel system, lower the jockey wheel on to the ground and re-tighten the clamp. If you wish, you can now manually lift the caravan coupling head clear of the car (vertebrae permitting) but in this case you would leave the caravan handbrake off since you will need to swing the nose of the van to one side, clear of the car's towball. Alternatively, raise the caravan coupling head by winding the jockey wheel handle until the coupling is raised clear of the towball, then move the car away. Do not forget to replace the plastic towball cover immediately, otherwise as soon as someone goes to unload the car boot they will get grease from the towball on their legs – I learnt this the hard way. (Being a bit dim, I still do it from time to time, earning the severe displeasure of Herself!)

Before detaching caravan from car you should consider which way you want it to face. Primarily you would consider the view from your caravan's front end, which is where you usually sit for meals etc. If you are also rigging an awning, the prevailing wind might be a consideration.

You may, of course, be on a more organised site than a farmer's field, and you could be required to site your caravan in the same way as your neighbour's. If you are on level ground, turning the caravan around only needs a bit of a push on the part of your family or perhaps helpful neighbours. Remember, though, that you cannot swing the caravan round with the handbrake applied.

Having sited the caravan, you wind down the corner steadies until the caravan rests firmly on all four corners. The steadies aren't designed to lift the wheels off the ground, but just to take some of the load and, as the word implies, to keep the caravan from rocking in a wind. A useful purchase is a small plastic triangle into which are set two spirit levels at right angles to each other. With this placed on a flat surface inside the caravan, you can adjust the corner steadies until the caravan is level, both side to side and fore and aft. This is essential if you have a fridge, since most fridges will not function with more than a 3° tilt. Additionally you could find, on washing up dishes, that the water on the draining board runs 'uphill' into the cooker (causing more displeasure from Herself)!

Towing on to blocks

If the ground slopes from one side of the caravan to the other, before detaching caravan from car you must tow it up on to some wooden blocks placed in front of the downhill wheel. I always carry one or two 8-inch long pieces of 4-inch × 2-inch or 4-inch × 3-inch timber to cope with sloping sites. You also need to carry four pieces of plank, ½-inch or ¾-inch thick, each about 6 inches long by 3 inches wide. These are to go under the corner steadies to prevent them sinking into the ground when you site the caravan.

As an alternative to towing the caravan up on to wooden blocks if one wheel is lower than the other, you can buy a levelling device which is a metal frame which you place in front of the lower wheel. You pull the caravan forward on to the frame and by turning the handle, or tommy bar, you can raise the wheel as necessary.

For easy checking on levels, there is an excellent device available called the 'Lambilevel'. This consists of a spirit level, some 6 inches long, which is mounted on the front end of the caravan where it can be clearly seen from inside the car. You can spot the moment, therefore, when your caravan is on a level plane from side to side. A second spirit level can be

The Lambilevel including Rev-aid reversing alignment indicator.
Photo courtesy of Howard Lambie.

attached to the drawbar of the caravan or the side of the gas cylinder locker in order to attain a fore and aft level, and finally a third one can be fixed to the rear end of the van for adjusting the rear corner steadies.

The Lambilevel was produced and marketed for many years by its inventor, Howard Lambie, an experienced caravanner and Caravan Club member. He has now retired but fortunately this excellent accessory had been taken over and is available from the new proprietors Selsmore (Marketing) Ltd. of Havant, Hants (see Useful Addresses.)

Perhaps a simpler alternative is a circular spirit level, where when the bubble is dead centre the caravan is level in all directions. This is available from Strawson Inclinometers Ltd (see Useful Addresses).

Checklist: Unhitching and Levelling

- Get the van positioned using the car – it's easier than pushing it (see Chapter 3 on reversing).

- Choose the site carefully: prevailing wind; position of sun; view; level; firm ground if possible; access; exit.

- Tow on to wood blocks to level, if necessary.

- Before unhitching van from car, jockey wheel must be down and clamped, and the caravan handbrake in 'on' position especially if one wheel is up on blocks. Detach stabilizer, brake safety chain and electrics. Finally detach caravan from car.

- Replace car towball cover *immediately* – or get greasy legs!

- Do not use corner steadies as jacks; they are to steady the caravan, *not* take the total weight.

- Get the van *level.*

Chapter 3

Reversing and Manoeuvring

Now we come to the oft-dreaded subject of reversing and manoeuvring. How easy it looks when you watch the skilled LGV driver reversing a 45-foot articulated lorry into a loading bay! Well the simple truth is that it is easier to reverse a big articulated lorry than a car and caravan, and I've done both.

The artic. has a short tractor and a long trailer which makes for easier reverse steering, whereas car and caravan are often the same length as each other. The extreme is reached when you try to reverse a little 5cwt camping trailer which is much shorter than the car. Don't try to practise reversing with such a set-up – the result is really discouraging. It 'jack-knifes' very easily!

Reversing to the Left

The first thing to grasp is that if you have caravan and car in a straight line, fore and aft, and you want to swing the back of the van round to the left while reversing, you must first turn the steering wheel to the *right*, ie the opposite of the normal drill for reversing the car solo.

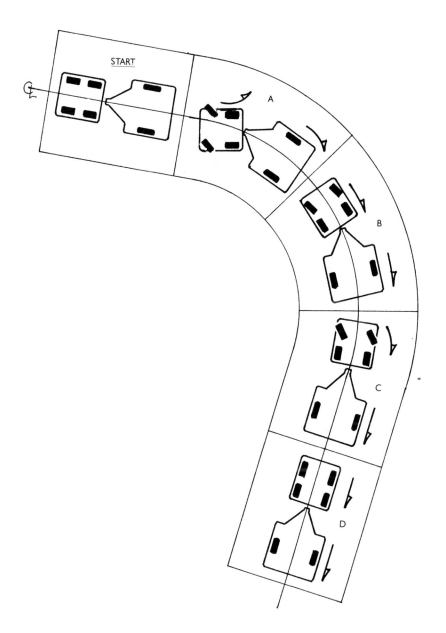

START

A

B

C

D

Figure 1   Reversing to the left

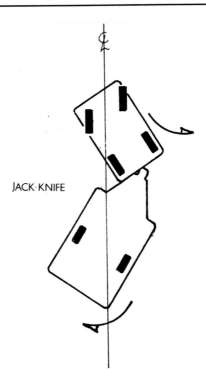

JACK-KNIFE

Figure 2   The jack-knife

The reason for this is as follows. On turning the steering wheel to the *right*, the back of the car (and towball) will swing to the *right* of the centre line, pushing the nose of the caravan also to the *right* of the centre line. The caravan will then pivot about its axle, and the rear of the caravan will swing to the *left* (see Figure 1(A)), which is what we are trying to achieve.

This is where disaster usually strikes, for if you keep the wheel to the right too long you will have the rear of the car and the front of the caravan both too far to the *right*. A little further like this and car and caravan will jack-knife, with the left side of the drawbar hard up against the left-hand rear end of the car (as in Figure 2), with both vehicles too far off the centre line, one to each side.

If we go back to Figure 1 (A), with the vehicles in the attitude shown, and immediately turn the steering wheel to the left – not too much – we arrive at a situation as shown in (B). Here the car is describing a gentle arc about the now curved centre line. The car is pushing the caravan with the front wheels at just the correct angle to maintain the curve. With very slight adjustments of the steering wheel you can maintain this curve until you have swung the whole outfit round as far as you want – perhaps through 90°. You must ensure that the angle between car and caravan does not increase, as it will if you tend to straighten the steering wheel, in which case you will again jack-knife as in Figure 2. This is because with the front wheels centred, the car will not follow our curve but the rear end will move over to the *right* of the curve. This will push the front of the caravan to the *right* of the curve, so that the rear of the van swings to the *left* of the curve and you collapse the outfit as in Figure 2.

Now the opposite of this last sequence is needed to straighten the outfit out, and run back in a straight line.

Assume we have curved round as far as we want to go (moving as in (B)), and we wish to go back in a straight line, as in the 'Start' figure. Turn the steering wheel further to the *left*. (This may take some believing since we're trying to straighten up – but be patient!) You can see from (C) that this swings the front of the car out to the *right* of our curved centre-line; *immediately* the front of the car has swung far enough to the right to be in a straight line with the caravan, turn the steering wheel to the right, back to *dead centre* as in (D). You are then running back again in a straight line.

Reversing to the Right

Reversing to the right is just the opposite of the above sequences.

Your side mirrors are essential for manoeuvring. As you go back in a straight line you should see equal amounts of caravan in each mirror. If you get an increased amount of van in your *right* mirror and it begins to disappear from your *left* mirror, turn the steering wheel slightly to the *right*. This will immediately correct the swing, but once the outfit is straight you must centre the wheel again. When reversing in a straight line, failure to correct the beginnings of a swing (ie when the caravan gets more prominent in one mirror or the other) will result eventually in a jack-knife.

Correcting a Jack-Knife

Now finally how to get out of a jack-knife, or any situation where the caravan is more to one side of the car than you intend. This is unbelievably simple. Stop, and go forward, centralising the steering wheel as you go. The car goes forward in a straight line, and quite simply the caravan follows. After literally a few yards your outfit is in a dead straight line, and you can get back to your intended manoeuvre.

Reversing in a Straight Line

Remember when reversing in a straight line, go slowly, and whichever side the caravan appears to increase in your mirrors, turn the wheel towards that side. Practise a bit on flat open ground or in a field. Try going straight back to begin with, using the above formula; then, using a few empty bottles or whatever, mark out a gentle curve and try your hand at this. You will soon get the hang of it – particularly if you can practise without an audience! It is very satisfying to be able to arrive on a site and put your caravan where you actually want it, and it really isn't difficult.

Automatic Reversing

Finally, modern caravans have an automatic reversing mechanism in the coupling gear; that is to say you can go astern without applying the caravan brakes. On older vans, you may need to get out of the car and operate a reversing catch to prevent locking the brakes as you start to reverse. It is now the law, however, that modern caravans must have automatic reversing mechanism.

Checklist: Reversing

● To reverse in a straight line use the side mirrors. On whichever side the caravan seems to show more, turn the steering wheel *towards* that side.

● To reverse round to the LEFT, start by turning the steering wheel to the RIGHT.

● Don't give up. *Practise!*

Chapter 4

Caravan Awnings

The subject of awnings was mentioned in Chapter 1, when your choice of caravan was discussed.

Provision of Additional Space

If you have a family I will repeat the advice to consider sleeping a couple of children – or adults – in an awning. This is a better consideration than buying a really large van to sleep everybody, which would be heavy, more expensive and need a bigger car to tow it. Even in a modest two-berth caravan, an awning can provide a spare bedroom. You would,

The Super Porch awning.

of course have an amicably prearranged system of signals, eg a gentle tap on the shoulder means 'you're snoring my darling'; two sharp shakes means 'you're still bloody well snoring'; and three violent shoves mean 'for God's sake push off and snore in the awning'. It's just like being at home really.

Awnings are freely available second-hand. Many dealers carry an excellent selection of awnings, both new and second-hand, in their special awning showroom – well worth a visit. Good value second-hand awnings are often to be seen advertised privately in the various caravan magazines. The Caravan Club's magazine *En Route* usually has a good selection. A couple of pages further on we will discuss how to make sure you get the correct size awning for your caravan.

Awnings come in many forms, sizes and materials. In recent years porch awnings have become popular and, as the name implies, they are fairly small and are rigged over the caravan door. Only a few feet in width and depth, they nevertheless provide weatherproof storage for folding chairs, welly boots, beach gear and so forth.

The Cabot awning.
Photo courtesy of ST Harrison Ltd.

Choice of Material

Full-size awnings are somewhat more ambitious and versatile. They are made, as are tents, either in heavy cotton canvas or synthetic materials. If it is necessary to strike camp in bad weather a wet awning is something of a liability. The canvas ones absorb a lot of water, are very heavy when wet, and must be spread and dried as soon as possible on reaching home, to avoid rot and mildew. Awnings made from canvas also need reproofing every couple of years or so once they are about four years old. Modern acrylic awnings tend to be a better buy, being rot proof and having a longer life. Synthetic materials will also suffer mildew when damp, however, although less so than cotton, and should also be thoroughly dried and aired as soon as possible.

Construction

Caravans today are fitted with an awning rail, which is an alloy channel fitted to the nearside of the caravan, running up one end, along the top and down the other end. The edge of the awning which joins the caravan finishes in a seam which

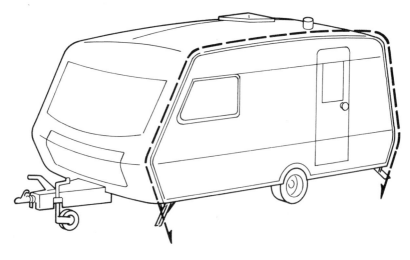

Awning channel

contains a plastic beading, to form a bolt-rope, and this is fed at one end into the end of the channel, and pulled right through around the caravan. This forms a secure and weather-proof joint between awning and van.

The awning is supported on a simple framework of poles, which can be of steel, alloy or even fibreglass to reduce weight. Clear plastic film windows, walls which roll up or zip out altogether, and small annexes to contain a chemical toilet are all available features, and of course space depends on the depth of the awning. On most modern caravans, except the basic ranges, there is an outside electric light on the awning side wall of the van, and so illumination at night in the awning is no problem. Plastic groundsheets are available, but as an economy measure a suitably sized piece of 1000 gauge polythene from a builders' merchant makes a good alternative.

Awning Sizes

Make sure you buy an awning which fits your van. They are loosely described as 'fit 12–13 foot van' which narrows things down a little, but the final measurement is important. This is known as the 'A' measurement, and it is the distance from the ground at one end of the caravan, vertically up through the awning channel, around the top of the van and down to the ground again at the other end. This is easily and accurately obtained by feeding a piece of string from the ground, up around the channel, and then measuring the string. This measurement is usually in centimetres, and for a 12 foot caravan will be something like 750–775 centimetres. It is important to get the measurement correct, since a 12 foot caravan is a 12 foot caravan, but the height of it can vary somewhat between different makes and so, therefore, can the ground-to-ground circumference. It is no good having a 6-inch gap between the ground and the bottom of the awning walls near the caravan.

Erecting the Awning

Before introducing the framework of poles the usual drill is to feed the bolt rope (the edge of the awning which joins to the

caravan) through the awning channel on the caravan. You will probably need to stand on the caravan step to do this.

Make sure you feed in the correct end first, depending on whether you feed from the front of the van or the rear, otherwise you will find you have the awning inside-out. If the end walls and roof of the awning are all in one piece, the whole thing must be fed through the channel at once. If end walls and roof are separate from each other, feed the roof section into the channel first, then erect the framework of poles and finally attach the end walls. This is done by feeding each wall up through the channel from the bottom and attaching the top of each wall to the roof – usually by means of a sturdy zip fastener.

In any event, erecting an awning is nearly always a two man job. When first attaching the fabric to the caravan, one person feeds the bolt rope into the channel while the other pulls the fabric along, and it is here that it is usually necessary to gain some extra height by standing on the caravan step. When the fabric is in place, either the whole awning or just the roof if the end walls are separate, one person holds up the roof from inside, while the other nips nimbly about, also inside, erecting the framework of poles.

The awning is finally secured by fastening down around the bottom edge with tent pegs. Normally additional guy ropes are not necessary, but these are a wise precaution in very windy conditions. If you site your outfit, perhaps at the coast where there is a strong prevailing wind, it is worth arranging things so that the awning is on the sheltered side of the caravan. In these conditions a stone wall or a clump of bushes can make an effective windbreak.

Include a mallet or a hammer in your tool kit – on some types of ground, tent pegs take some knocking in! They are available in either plastic or steel.

Finally, a word on poles. On new awnings the poles will collapse down into short lengths on spring-loaded connections. In the case of secondhand poles, some may have perhaps parted company from their neighbouring section, so you have a number of short sections that don't seem to have a home. Even on a new awning where the pole joins are intact, this bag-full of poles lies on the ground in a meaningless jumble, defying you to assemble them without having several bits left over.

Reference to the maker's hand-out may or may not help. These instructions often seem to be written by someone specially recruited from a Government 'confusing pamphlet' department. More than once with a new awning we have stood in a field, longing for a drink, surrounded by a jumble of defiant looking poles, while it steadily grew dark and began to rain. As I have said before, I am a bit dim – happily, Herself is an expert at mastering the puzzle, and the awning is up in no time.

The moral is to get the dealer, or previous owner, to show you how the poles assemble. The (usually) three horizontal poles supporting the roof of the awning have to join the side of the caravan along the side wall. This is sometimes achieved by having rubber 'sucker' cups on the ends of the poles. These are not really satisfactory, and on a caravan with a 'crimpled' surface are useless. A better joint is obtained with plastic eyes screwed to the caravan, with plastic hooks to engage them on the ends of the poles. Packs of these awning fittings are available from most caravan dealers. Remember, any hole bored into a caravan wall must be well sealed to prevent water entering.

When you put your awning up for the first time, identify each section of frame and mark it with masking tape, which is easy to write on. Once familiar with the poles, you should part-assemble them, and lay them out on the ground around the intended site for the awning, where each one will be required, ie left side, right side, front etc. Do this even before you feed the fabric into the awning channel. All this is not nearly as difficult as it sounds, and once you've done it a couple of times it becomes very simple. We can have our awning up in about five minutes and, by the time I have pegged down the walls, Herself has produced a pot of tea and the tentative suggestion that perhaps the whole outfit might be better off just a couple of yards further to the right?

Checklist: Awnings

- Secondhand awnings are a good buy. Most dealers keep a selection.

- Know the size required. The vital statistic is the ground-to-ground measurement – in centimetres. (Ground level up around the awning rail or channel on the caravan and back to ground level.)

- Synthetic fabrics are probably more practical than cotton.

- Identify and label with masking tape the sections of frame.

- Make up some extra guy ropes with really sturdy pegs, or some sort of earth anchors, for really stormy weather.

- Invest in a groundsheet, if only of builders' polythene.

- Do dry and air thoroughly as soon as possible if the awning has been packed away when wet.

Chapter 5

Equipment and Accessories

General Needs

Even the most luxurious caravan will not offer total comfort by itself and so in your 'payload' you must include basic obvious items such as gas cylinders, batteries, water containers (unless the van boasts a built-in water tank), the essential spare wheel, jack, step, chocks, some form of spirit level, plus cooking pots and pans, crockery, cutlery, glasses, tin opener, corkscrews, bedding, pillows, tea towels and washing-up gear, towels for the beach and bathroom, toilet kit, personal clothing including macs and wellies, books, games, children's toys, a torch, folding chairs, sunbeds and so on. Last but not least include a first-aid kit, sewing kit, tool kit and fire-fighting equipment.

Some of these items need no comment; some are worth a few words. They all contribute to total weight, and we will consider shortly just how much they add up to. Do save weight where possible – small savings here and there add up to quite a lot when considering the total.

Kitchen Utensils

An excellent set of nesting aluminium pans with removable handles is available. They have a non-stick finish (which on ours has now nearly disappeared but we have had them for many years and they have more than paid for themselves). When stacked they take up very little room and weight is minimal. We have a kettle and teapot made of aluminium, again of minimal weight. Crockery should preferably be of lightweight melamine, available from any caravan dealer's accessory shop – lightweight, colourful and easy to clean, they are virtually unbreakable. Drinking glasses also are available in clear plastic, in quite a variety of shapes and again light and unbreakable.

Bedding

This is a matter of choice and expediency. Particularly for children, sleeping bags are the obvious answer, lightweight, easy to make up and stow away. Two sleeping bags can be zipped together to make a double, but sleeping bags don't suit everyone. We ourselves don't like being confined at sides or bottom end, so we often make up a conventional bed with sheets and blankets. Our two-berth van has an ample, comfortable bed about 6.5 feet square. However, it is a tedious business folding up sheets and blankets every morning, and re-making the bed at night, so the ideal answer is probably a bottom blanket and sheet topped by an un-zipped sleeping bag used in the role of a duvet. Sleeping bags should not be too heavy.

Clothing

Items of personal clothing should be kept to a minimum – it adds up in terms of weight and volume at an alarming rate, You obviously don't need much in the way of guernseys and thermal underwear if you're making for the Mediterranean in August, but nearer home some warm clothing should be taken. There is nothing more miserable than being cold.

If you are going to an established site in the summer, there are usually laundry rooms. We are not really into heavy laundry sessions when on holiday, but rinsing out lightweight shirts, tops and underwear is a simple enough matter in the caravan. You can usually rig up a short clothes line, or you can buy a folding rack which clips on to an open caravan window ledge and is ideal for drying 'smalls', tea towels, etc. I can promise you that you won't wear half the clothes you take with you, so keep the wardrobe list short.

First Aid

A good medical/first-aid kit is essential. You can make up one for yourself with a little thought. We carry ours clearly marked in a plastic ice cream container, with lid. Apart from the obvious first-aid items, carry some disinfectant, remedies for

upset stomachs, and some insect repellent plus sting relief cream for insect bites. A chemist will gladly advise you on what to include.

If going abroad, some water purifying tablets are worth using. They are available from dealers and are a wise precaution against the sometimes questionable drinking water found on some sites abroad.

Fire Fighting Equipment

A fire extinguisher is something I hope you will never need, but if you do need it then you need it badly! Would you really take that chance just to save a few pounds? (£s or lbs.) You need the dry powder type of extinguisher which is usually available in the minimum recommended 1kg size; it comes with a quick-release mounting bracket and should be sited near the exit door. With constant towing the dry powder in an extinguisher can settle and become compacted. Take it out of its holding bracket occasionally, invert it and tap it a few times to keep the contents loose.

We also carry a fire blanket which – unlike an extinguisher – lasts forever (if unused!). This is usually kept near the kitchen in case of a cooking pan fire. It really is better to be safe than sorry.

On the subject of fire, *all* new vans sold after 1 March 1990, and indeed a number sold before then, will have upholstery containing Combustion Modified High Resilience Foam (CMHR), to avoid the dense toxic smoke given off by the older stuff. Additionally, from April 1991, the actual furnishing fabrics will be fire-resistant.

For older caravans with pre fire-resistant upholstery, a very useful flame retardant spray is available from the Humbrol paint people. Spray it on furnishing fabrics, curtains, etc. Long lasting and non-staining, it is available from DIY stores.

Smoke Alarms

As from 1 May 1989 all new vans, *and second-hand vans sold through a dealer*, will have been fitted with a smoke alarm.

These smoke detectors will differ from the ordinary domestic version, in that there will be a facility for switching them to a lower key or less sensitive mode for a short period of a few minutes, while the caravanner takes a shower, cooks toast or bacon or whatever, since these activities within the confines of a caravan would trigger off a normal domestic smoke alarm. This modification is important, since one must avoid a situation where a caravanner becomes irritated by false alarms to the point where batteries are removed, or the detector is taken down and stuffed out of sight in a bedding locker.

Payload

We talked earlier about the 'payload' of the van, which was the difference between the ex-works weight of the van and its Maximum Laden Weight (or Maximum Gross Weight). We also said we wanted to keep below the very maximum permitted level so that our Actual Laden Weight was somewhat less than the specified MLW. The ALW therefore, is the weight of the bare van plus everything we load into it – in other words, all the stuff we've listed in this chapter. So how much do all these things weigh?

Here is a list of weights, some of them only approximate since, for example, the weight of an awning will depend on its size and type of material and poles.

Weights of Equipment

Item	Weight (in lbs)
Awning (porch)	30
Awning (full)	45
Butane cylinder (10lbs size)	12 empty; 22 full
(7 kg size)	18 empty; 33 full
Battery (depending on size)	35
Spare wheel	30
Chemical toilet (empty)	15
Fridge	30 (could be up to 60)
Oven	34

Item	Weight (in lbs)
Melamine crockery/cutlery; glasses; alloy cooking pots	20
Fire extinguisher and blanket	4
Wood blocks and chocks	10
Bedding (per person approx.)	10
Clothing (per person approx.)	25
Books and games (approx)	12
Folding chair (lightweight)	4
First-aid kit	2

Allowing for two full 10-lb size gas cylinders, a full awning, clothing and bedding for three people, these items total about 3½ cwt or 392 lbs, depending on the size of fridge. However, the fridge should be allowed for by the van manufacturer when calculating your payload. Also, much of your personal luggage (quite a heavy item) will normally go in the car rather than in the caravan. I usually stow the awning in the car and this accounts for a fair weight. Against this there are various items not listed above, such as two 5-gallon water containers plus one waste water container. However, these and various other small items amount only to a few pounds in weight.

We are talking of approximately 3 cwt of gear to be loaded, therefore, and it should not be difficult to settle on a caravan which can accept this, and conform with the target weights we have discussed earlier. You must do your own sums which will depend to a great extent on the size of your party and your car. Do be aware of your limits. Do *not* overload, ie do *not* exceed your MLW. Also do *not* accept the manufacturer's ex-works weight as gospel; it is quite often inaccurate. It may legally vary by up to plus or minus 5 per cent. Find a public weighbridge and weigh the caravan empty – or better still, loaded up with all your gear.

Finally, you will have to be prepared to do your sums in metric amounts. We are currently in the middle of a sort of twilight zone wherein what is left of the civilised world is steadily being bullied into centigrade, litres, kilometres, hectares, kilojoules and God knows what. Personally at my age I want none of it. I mean, imagine asking for 570 millilitres of Guinness! Meaningless. However, one cannot hold out against progress for ever, and we shall increasingly be calculating our caravan loading in kilos. At present we are at the rather confusing halfway stage of dealing with both Imperial and metric, and that's without coping with Welsh or Cornish. If, like me, you are almost eligible for Dame Edna's Maximum Security Home for the Totally Bewildered, you might like a repeat of the little conversion table we gave in chapter 1, in a slightly simpler form. So, to help you with your sums, remember:

$$1 \text{ kilogramme} = 2.2 \text{ lbs}$$
$$1 \text{lb} = 0.45 \text{ kg.}$$

Checklist: Equipment and luggage

- Keep weight *down*.

- Use lightweight cooking pots and crockery.

- Don't take more clothing than you need.

- First-aid outfit, fire extinguisher and fire blanket are top priority.

- Save weight wherever possible. A few ounces here and half a pound there add up to a significant amount when you total all the stuff you want to include.

- Don't expect to get it right first time.

- Don't overburden yourself with gadgets. Accessory shops encourage impulse buying!

Chapter 6

Water Supply

Containers

Any system of running water in the caravan, simple or sophisticated, depends on a supply of water to the van and this, in turn, usually depends on your actually getting it there. Let us consider therefore the best way of fetching it. A simple site such as a Caravan Club certificated location or a Camping and Caravanning Club 'hideaway' will probably have just one tap – either in the field itself or even in the farmyard, which might mean fetching the water in the car. A permanent site catering for a considerable number of vans will have water points about the location, so you won't have to go very far. The more water you can fetch at one go, obviously the less frequently you will have to make the trek.

I am often surprised at the odd collection of vessels which people use for carrying water, some so small that a couple of pots of tea will empty them which is quite impractical.

There are two main types of worthwhile container: first, the lightweight plastic 'jerrican' with a screw cap, holding five gallons. Anything bigger than this is really too heavy to lift, since five gallons weighs 50lbs. The second type is a circular plastic drum which holds about six gallons; it has a handle which clips on to each end, and the container is rolled along looking for all the world like a garden roller. A well known example is the 'Aquaroll'. When empty, these are heavier and bulkier than the rectangular jerrican type.

I have always used two plastic rectangular cans in conjunction with a wheeled carrier. This is a simple but clever little trolley with two wheels, which holds one five-gallon container and which collapses flat for stowage. The same trolley also accommodates the waste tank of our cassette chemical toilet. A most useful piece of gear.

The reason for having two 5 gallon containers is that when the one in use runs dry, you are always in the middle of

The Aquaroll water container.
Photo courtesy of F. L. Hitchman.

making coffee, washing up or having a shower. You don't want to break off and trek across the field for a refill. It's better to nip out and change to the full container, and then get a refill later. This is my argument against the 'rollalong' type, you still need two of them and they are really bulky. Using two containers; I find that ten gallons will last the two of us a little over 24 hours, give or take half a day.

81

Plumbing

Having got your bulk supply to the caravan, what's next? Here, let me point out that water systems, along with other services, have changed considerably over the past few years. Later in this chapter we discuss modern submersible electric pumps which are now found on most new caravans, and some larger vans also boast inboard water tanks. Many caravans are still available with far less sophisticated plumbing, however, and we look at these first.

The caravan will have two fixed rigid plastic spouts, located underneath and a few inches in from the edge of the van. One of these connects, via plastic tubing, to the outlets or taps in the caravan, and the other connects to sink and washbasin outlets and deals with waste water. You cannot connect fresh water inlet or waste outlet by mistake, since the inlet spout connects to ½-inch supply tubing, and the waste spout to ¾-inch.

While touching on the subject of waste, you need a third five-gallon container for waste, plus a foot or so of ¾-inch plastic hose to connect the waste spout to the container. You won't be able to stand the waste container upright, as it would stand above the level of the outlet spout on the caravan. It must be laid flat and you must cut a small hole on the flat side of the waste container – close to what is the top of the container when it stands upright. Alternatively, you can buy a five-gallon container specially designed for waste. These are usually black in colour; they have a ¾-inch spout on the side near the top, so that you can connect your short length of ¾-inch hose from the van outlet to the container.

It is surprising, with washing up water and personal ablutions, how quickly the waste container fills up. It must be emptied regularly, and on an organised site there will be waste water disposal points near the fresh water supply – don't just dump it on the nearest patch of grass.

Waste containers soon collect a disgusting lining of grease and general gunge, and after a period of use they should be thoroughly cleaned. Put in handfuls of sharp sand or gravel and a few pints of very hot water plus a little detergent, and give the whole thing a good shaking. Treat with disinfectant after rinsing it clean.

Returning to the subject of fresh water, having fetched your containers of water stand them next to the caravan near the fresh water connection. This will be either at the rear or the side of the caravan, depending on whether the van has an end or side kitchen. You must connect the inlet to the container with a length of ½-inch plastic hose. Don't just drop the hose into the container, however; the comparatively soft hose will tend to curl up and the end would then finish halfway up the inside of the container, so that you would only be able to pump out half the water. Fix the plastic hose to a length of rigid ½-inch plastic tube, which will pass through a rubber bung which fits the filling hole on the container. This will keep out insects, but make sure you have a breather hole in the bung otherwise a vacuum will form in the container, preventing water from being pumped out. Do use a jubilee clip to fasten the plastic hose to the rigid pipe which goes into the container. Failure to make an airtight joint here will allow air to be sucked into the supply, and your pump will not function. Rigid pipes and bungs are available from any caravan dealer.

You now have your full container connected to the caravan. In an older caravan of the type we are discussing, water is pumped up by a foot pump which fits flush with the caravan floor and is located near the kitchen sink. On a simple system the water is pumped up and emerges through the outlet into the sink. Additionally you could have a 12-volt electric pump to supplement the foot pump. The foot pump is still neces-sary, however, since after connecting the water container outside the caravan, the water has to be sucked up, and since the foot pump has a diaphragm action it is self-priming and will draw water up from the container. The electric pump is simply an impeller and is not self-priming, but once the system is primed the electric pump will continue to function until a fresh container is brought into use, when the system has to be re-primed with the foot pump.

It is worth carrying a small selection of washers and spares for the water foot pump if you have one. These can usually be obtained as a kit. Keep a couple of jubilee clips to cope with pipe maintenance.

The next step up from one outlet to the kitchen sink is a second one to the wash basin in the toilet compartment. If one is not already fitted to your caravan it is not difficult to do it yourself. At a convenient place on the top side of the pump (or pumps) a 'Y' joint is fitted into the plastic hose, using jubilee clips. A length of hose is led to the wash basin, terminating in an outlet fitting. This must now have a tap to cut off the flow, as must the first outlet in the kitchen otherwise when the pump is operated, water will flow from both outlets at once. All these water installation accessories, such as plastic hose, jubilee clips, plastic 'Y' joints and so on, can be supplied by a caravan dealer.

You can obtain taps which are wired electrically so that, when turned on, the connection is made to the 12-volt electric pump, and water flows as required.

It is probably worth mentioning the system we used on an earlier caravan to avoid switching our supply pipe from container to container when one was empty.

About two feet along the pipe, between the caravan and the water container, I installed a plastic 'Y' joint, and from there I led two pipes, each ending in the rigid plastic tube and rubber bung where the tubes enter the two five-gallon containers. We therefore drew water from both containers simultaneously, which avoided the changeover when one was empty. I fitted a non-return valve to the lower end of each rigid tube, so that when the tubes were withdrawn from the empty containers they remained full. I could then insert them into the re-filled containers without having to re-prime the system with the footpump. When you did run dry however, you had two containers to fill.

On any joints you make when modifying your water system do use jubilee clips. A tightish push-fit won't do. Water gets out and air gets in, and that spells trouble and pump mal-function.

Hot Water (Gas Heated)

Now that we have a cold water supply to the two consumer points, the next refinement is hot running water. Two main types of installation can provide this. The earlier type, which we had installed in two previous caravans, works like the domestic Ascot gas heater. The gas-fired unit is fixed to a

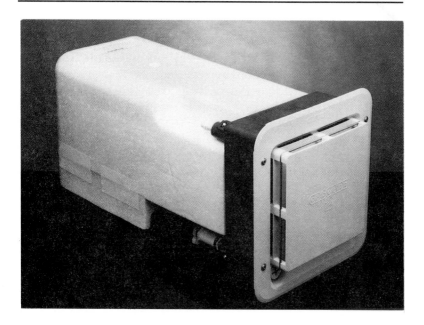

The Cascade 2 storage water heater.

convenient wall, cold water is routed into it from the pump and hot water routed from it to the separate hot water tap or taps. The unit is also connected to the gas supply system. This is usually done by inserting a 'T' joint into the copper gas supply pipe between the gas cylinder and cooker, and taking a branch to the heater.

In this system, as water is pumped through at a given pressure, the burners ignite and heat the water as it passes through, thus generating considerable heat, which escapes through the top of the unit. This is one disadvantage, and it may be necessary to fit some sort of sheet aluminium shield above the unit to avoid scorching the roof of the caravan. There might also be a problem in pumping cold water through the heater at sufficient pressure to activate the gas supply to the burners. We did have a problem here until I discovered that the fault occurred when drawing electric power from the car. Voltage drop over the long route from the car battery caused the electric pump to produce insufficient water pressure to activate the burners. Switching to the caravan battery as the power source solved the problem.

It should be noted that some of these heaters need an external flue.

This method of heating water immediately prior to delivering has now been superseded by a more efficient system, which operates in a similar way to a household domestic storage system and is a standard feature of most new caravans. Water is heated by a gas burner with an external flue, located under the floor of the caravan. There is therefore no problem with superfluous heat or gas fumes. After heating, the water is stored in a lagged copper tank which is usually located in a locker under one of the forward seats.

The system we have is the 'Carver Cascade'. Hot water is piped to the hot water tap or taps, and as cold water is pumped into the bottom of the storage tank, hot water is forced out of the top and along to the taps. When the temperature of water in the tank drops, a thermostatic control switches on the under-floor burner until the desired temperature is again reached. The system is very efficient, economical and safe. Any fault in either gas, water or electricity supply causes the fail-safe mechanism to shut down the unit, and a warning light is displayed on the separate control panel which can be located in any convenient position in the caravan. They are sensitive to voltage drop and need a minimum 10.5 volts to operate.

Even the Carver 'Cascade' hot water storage system is within the scope of a competent DIY person. The kit comes with very clear instructions. Let me stress again that if you have modified your gas supply piping, do get your dealer to do a pressure test afterwards, to check for leaks. Whichever type of hot water system you have, do drain the heater for the winter, unless your caravan is in frost-proof storage. (I didn't bother one year, and frost damage gave me a repair bill I could well have done without!)

Hot Water (Electrically Heated)

The Carver Cascade 2 (2 denotes 2-gallon storage capacity) described in the previous section has now been developed to produce a water heater with a dual power source, ie gas and mains electricity.

The Cascade GE works in its gas powered mode just as the Cascade 2 does, but also contains a mains electric immersion heater. This will operate off 220/240 volts, and its current consumption on 240 volts is a modest 2.7 amps. This low consumption means that it will take about 55 minutes to produce hot water, but if gas and electricity are used simultaneously, hot water is available in about 20 minutes. Once heated, the two-gallon storage tank is easily kept at operating temperature by either of the power sources.

On sites with mains electricity, the immersion heater is another contribution to saving gas. Without doubt this dual power water heater is a real step forward, and is certain to be standard equipment in the well-appointed caravan.

For older caravans, but those which have had mains electricity installed, there is a neat electric water heater available which is simpler and cheaper than a full gas water heating system. This is the 'Elgena KB3' unit, which can be obtained through Bicknacre Caravan and Leisure (see Useful Addresses). It is a simple and compact device, easy to install, and it holds and heats three litres of water at a time.

Submersible Pumps

So far this chapter has largely dealt with what now seem to be essentially primitive water supply systems. There are, and will be for years to come, caravans on which these basic systems are found.

All this has now been radically changed by the arrival of the 12 volt submersible pump, which usually operates in conjunction with the gas or gas/mains electric hot water storage system. The two appliances have raised caravan water supply almost to the level of modern domestic plumbing. The submersible pump has completely done away with the need for the old foot pump. Carver again are the principal suppliers and the system is called the 'Crystal', although other popular makes are available. Simply expressed, it consists of a flexible roll-up hose with an electric impeller pump at its lower end. The wire to the pump runs down the hose, and the pump at the end of the hose is lowered to the bottom of the water container, where it pumps water up and into the caravan's

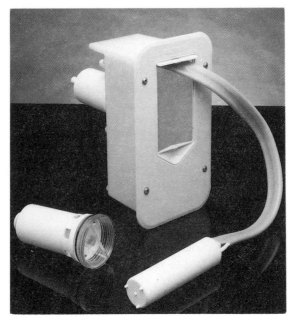

The Crystal water system.
Photo courtesy of Carver & Co (Engineers) Ltd.

water circuit. When not in use the compact pump and hose are rolled up and housed in a small locker in the outside wall of the caravan. The van's water system is routed from the inside of this locker. The compact submersible pump system incorporates a filter containing carbon granules. This filter should be renewed every year. The system does away with having to connect a supply pipe from the container to an inlet connection on the underside of the caravan. More significantly, since the pump is actually submerged in the supply container it does not require priming, so the foot pump becomes redundant.

One still ideally needs two separate water containers, to enable a quick and easy changeover to be made when one container runs dry without warning.

A year after the Carver 'Crystal' was first exhibited at the Caravan Show at Earls Court most new caravans, other than those with essentially basic specifications, were supplied fitted with the system and without foot pumps. As long as you have a reliable source of electric power this is fine. A submersible pump can, of course, freeze up in a water container located outside in sub-zero temperatures. For a long time to come, however, there will be older caravans where the plastic hose connection from container to van is necessary.

Pressurised water systems

When electric submersible pumps were first introduced, they were activated by micro switches located in the body of each tap, and the action of turning on a tap completed the circuit and the pump operated. If the caravan had a shower there were probably six taps altogether, hence six separate micro switches, which are not always reliable. Pump failure due to faulty micro switches is not uncommon, and is most annoying.

The problem has been largely solved by the introduction of pressurised water systems. Briefly this works more like a domestic system. The pump isolator switch is turned on, the pump functions and water pressure builds up in the system. Turning a tap on will obviously cause water to flow. When the tap is turned off, however, the pump continues to function until the pressure in the pipe system reaches a given level, which can be somewhere between 15 and 30 psi. (This is adjustable.) When this pressure is reached, a pressure sensitive diaphragm operates the only switch in the system and the pump is switched off. The system remains pressurised and as soon as a tap is turned on again, water will flow. This then relieves the pressure and as it drops, the diaphragm again activates the switch, the pump starts up and the system works as before.

It is worth noting that it is advisable, after a bout of washing up or showering, to turn off the pump isolator switch. This is because a leak or a loose pipe connection will allow the water pressure to drop, thus activating the pump which will quietly go on flooding your caravan until the container is empty. Unlikely in a well maintained van, but by no means impossible. Sureflo and Whale are two well known manufacturers of pressurised water equipment.

On any joints you make when modifying your water system, do use jubilee clips. A tightish push-fit won't do. Water gets out and air gets in, and that spells trouble and pump malfunction.

Inboard water tanks

Larger modern vans may be fitted with a built in fresh water tank, so there is no question of dropping a submersible pump into a water container standing alongside the van. The inboard tank can be filled in one of two ways. If you are near enough to the supply point, a hose can be used to fill the tank, which has a filler cap as on a car petrol tank. Failing this, one still has to fetch water in a container.

The caravan may have a small 12 volt socket on the outside, near the tank filler point, in which case one needs a submersible pump with a short length of hose and a similar length of wire plus plug. The water can then be pumped into the tank, which usually has a fairly large capacity. A submersible pump plus hose and wire can be found in any caravan accessory shop. We use exactly this method to fill the flushing tank of our Thetford cassette toilet, which is filled from outside the van.

The inboard fresh water tank will usually have a constant displacement pump to supply the various taps, shower etc. in the caravan. Such a pump will run whether the tank is full or dry, whereas a submersible pump which is dropped into an outside water container will suffer damage if run dry.

Checklist: Water Supply

- Use five-gallon plastic containers, or an 'Aquaroll'. Small containers are useless.

- Buy a small water trolley – it saves a lot of work.

- Use Jubilee clips, *fitted tightly*, on all hose connections.

- On older vans with manual or foot-operated pumps, keep a spare set of washers, diaphragm etc.

- To install a hot water system use correct high-temperature hose (coloured red).

- Sterilise the whole system annually. (See Chapter 15, on maintenance.)

- On submersible (impeller) pumps, replace the carbon filter annually. This is important, since bacteria will grow in an old filter cartridge.

- *Remember* – drain any water heater before the winter lay-up.

Chapter 7

Sanitation

Chemical Toilet

Whether or not you carry a chemical toilet in your caravan depends on whether you will spend all your time on sites with toilet facilities. Caravan Club certificated locations and Camping and Caravanning Club 'hideaways' (five vans only and usually in a farmer's field) require you to have your own toilet facilities. Most, though not all, permanent sites whether club sites or commercial will have at least one toilet block. Even so, do you or your family want to face the task of occasionally trekking, perhaps through the rain, a quarter of a mile or so at 3.00am?

Assuming you do carry your own toilet, where will you locate it? There are three options: in the toilet compartment in the van or, secondly, in a separate toilet tent (which is a small tent, like a miniature telephone kiosk, about three feet square). A third option would be to have an awning which has a toilet annex – virtually a toilet tent but built into the body of the awning.

All chemical toilets are used with a special chemical fluid, which is widely obtainable from caravan dealers and often site shops. This is usually a blue-coloured liquid which breaks down and sterilises solid waste matter and also acts as an effective deodorant.

The toilet unit itself can vary from very simple to quite sophisticated. In its simplest form a chemical toilet consists of a container with a seat and a lid. A step up from this involves an inner bucket or container which can be removed for emptying, and the lid forms a tight seal which keeps the contents where they should be when the caravan is on the move. Ideally, of course, the toilet should be emptied before moving on.

Two-tank toilet

A few years ago there was a great step forward with the introduction of two-tank toilets. These consist of a lower storage tank, above which is a conventional toilet bowl surmounted by a seat and a lid. Separating the two compartments is a simple valve which slides sideways to open or close. Around the outside of the upper bowl is a tank containing fresh water with which the bowl can be flushed by using a neat hand pump or, on some models, an electric pump. The whole outfit comes apart, the upper bowl and flushing tank lifting clear of the holding tank. The latter only, with the valve closed, is then taken to the disposal point, and is emptied through a convenient spout which swivels out from the top of the tank. The great advantage of the two-tank variety is the ease of emptying plus the fact that in use the contents of the lower tank remain out of sight.

Cassette Toilet

Among the best known of these two-tank toilets is the range produced under the 'Porta Potti' name. However, the ultimate in caravan toilets, which is now standard equipment on many vans, is the Thetford 'Cassette Porta Potti'. The main part of the toilet incorporating the bowl, flushing-water holding tank and flushing pump is a permanent fixture in the caravan's toilet compartment. The 'cassette' part is the waste-holding tank which slides out sideways from under the assembly through a small trapdoor in the side of the caravan. Even the flushing-water tank is refilled from outside the van. As with some of the portable models there is a level indicator to prompt the emptying of the holding tank. The flushing-water tank also has a level gauge. It goes without saying, of course, that the waste tank should only be removed for emptying when the toilet is not in use!

This thought evoked a dim memory from the days when I was soldiering in the Middle East. The loos I remember were a simple corrugated iron structure (with an inside temperature of about 130°F). There was a rigid wooden seat, with bucket beneath, which was withdrawn through a trapdoor in the rear

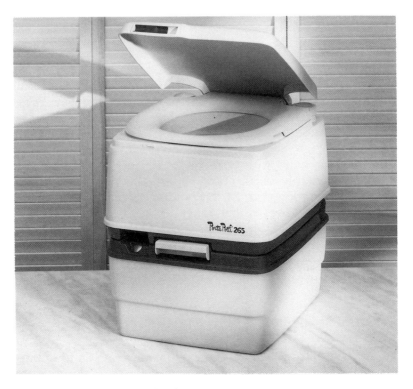

The Porta Potti 265 two-tank toilet.

of the outfit for disposal. Sadly, the local sanitary operative would frequently whip open the trapdoor and remove the bucket regardless of whether the facilities were actually in use at the time. This could prove inconvenient, to say the least, and at times even painful.

While on the subject of 'conveniences', I vividly recall a unique piece of military plumbing at a dreadful and primitive camp somewhere in Kent. A communal affair, it consisted of a long piece of 18-inch drainpipe laid along the ground with holes cut along the top at 3-foot intervals, with simple wooden seats attached. Hessian partitions separated one from one's neighbour, but you could sit there and view the rolling Kent countryside in panoramic splendour. This appliance was flushed by discharging a 500 gallon water tank along it at hourly intervals.

The Cassette Porta Potti.
Photo courtesy of Thetford (Aqua) Products Ltd.

There was always a certain level of water in the pipe, however, and much innocent merriment was to be had by loosely bunching up a wad of newspaper, igniting it and floating it along beneath your neighbour, whereupon, there would be cries of 'dear oh dear' and 'oh you bounder', and other abusive expressions.

The principal attraction of this apparatus, however, lay in its flushing mode. When the 500 gallons was on its way, a distant roaring noise could be heard and the more experienced 'campers' would leap clear. Before the wall of water arrived it was preceded by such a draught of wind that, with skilled

personnel rising and sitting in concert as it were, the whole thing could be played like a vast clarinet. Unfortunately no record of this phenomenon appears in any war diary, which is a pity – it was quite unique.

But I digress. As I said in discussing the excellent Thetford Cassette Porta Potti, just make sure you don't set about emptying it while it is in use. Perhaps some form of whistle signals could be agreed upon!

Checklist: Sanitation

- Larger and established sites generally have toilets. Certificated locations and hideaways (often farm locations) do not.

- Caravan toilets are of three types. The basic ones have a bucket plus a seat. Much better are twin-tank toilets. The most superior type has a seat and flushing tank permanently built into the caravan, and a cassette-type waste tank which is withdrawn from outside through a trap door.

- All three need a chemical toilet fluid.

- Except for the cassette type you keep the toilet either in the caravan loo compartment or a separate toilet tent, or in a toilet compartment built onto the awning. There are advantages and disadvantages with all three.

- After a holiday in the caravan, wash out and disinfect the toilets. Leave valves, filler caps, etc open to allow air to circulate.

Chapter 8

Gas Supply

Gas

Cooking and heating depend on gas, as do the fridge and the water heater. We saw in Chapter 6, however, that where mains electricity is available, there are various ways of electrically heating your water. Similarly, most fridges will run on mains current.

With a modern caravan fridge, there are usually three options: 12 volt electricity, mains electricity or LPG (gas). The 12 volt facility is strictly for use on the move, when the moving tow car is supplying the 12 volt current. When stationary, a fridge running on 12 volt current will knock the stuffing out of the battery in a very short time.

Using mains current for fridge and water heater undoubtedly makes for worthwhile savings in gas. Electric cooking can be considered using a microwave, but do heed the reference to microwaves on page 127.

Back to gas – Liquified Petroleum Gas (LPG). Butane is more common, but propane may be used. The essential difference is that propane will function at much lower temperatures than butane, and is really necessary for mid-winter caravanning when it can become too cold for butane to flow freely. It should be noted that butane and propane require different types of regulator. A regulator is fitted to the gas cylinder and ensures that, regardless of the volume of fuel in the cylinder, gas is supplied to the appliances at a constant uniform pressure.

The principal fuel sources are either Camping Gaz, Calor gas or Shell. Calor gas and Shell supply propane and butane, Camping gaz only supply butane. Camping Gaz is supplied throughout many Western European countries, Calor gas only in the UK. Butane is in blue cylinders, propane in red, though some smaller distributors may use other colours.

You should decide on and stick to one brand, since each

has its own type of regulator and fittings and they are not interchangeable. However, there is widely available an adaptor which permits a Calor gas regulator to be used with Camping Gaz if you should run out of Calor gas when abroad. We have caravanned in France for years, and two of the small size (10lb) Calor gas cylinders have always lasted us through a 16-day holiday, and allowed us to cook and run a gas fridge and a water heater.

There are larger Calor gas containers available and you should be able to take enough gas abroad with you to cope with anything other than an extra-long holiday, or a large family. Again, decide which size to go for, since the 10lb size and the 7kg size have different regulator fittings.

You will have to pay for the hire of your first two cylinders outright; thereafter empty ones are exchanged for full ones, for just the price of the gas. It is usual to carry two cylinders so that you always have a full spare.

Calor gas is easily obtainable throughout the UK at caravan

A 7kg Calor butane cylinder fitted with 182H switch-on regulator.
Photo courtesy of Calor Gas Ltd.

dealers, many garages and hardware shops and, of course, at organised camp sites. You are not in fact buying the cylinders, only renting them. You should keep your rental receipt in case you wish to hand the cylinders back.

Every year you keep a Calor cylinder, the amount of your hire deposit which is returned to you goes down. At seven years, the refundable amount has dropped to 25 per cent, and it remains at that level for 50 years.

Cylinders are usually located in the caravan at the front end. On older vans there were a couple of clamps to locate the containers on the drawbar. From here they were fairly easily stolen, or vandals or evil kids could turn off (or on) the supply tap as the mood took them.

The next stage was a fibreglass locker located on the drawbar which accommodated two gas cylinders plus some-times a 12-volt battery (although the battery is better stored in the caravan, not with gas cylinders).

Jumbo-size lockers soon followed which, in addition to gas and battery, could accept a spare wheel and even an awning. This solves some major stowage problems but since these are together the four heaviest items to be carried, there is now a weight problem. The extreme front end of the van is possibly not the best place for all these items unless one keeps careful track of the resultant nose weight. These gas lockers are capable of being secured (after a fashion) with a small padlock, and are at least reasonably childproof.

More recently, with the advent of aerodynamic vans with sloping fronts, gas lockers have been located in a recess at the front, but built into the van itself with access via a flap or door lying flush with the van front. On some larger vans this principle has been used to locate a gas locker along the side, projecting into the caravan, possibly in the wardrobe. From the viewpoint of having the extra weight near the axle, this is good, although perversely it could result in insufficient noseweight for stable towing.

With the introduction of new safety standards which relate to LPG and electricity, all caravan manufacturers are required, since 1990, to keep the gas cylinders separate from the battery locker and from electric cable runs.

When the final parts of BS 6765 are in force (1994 at the latest) all gas rings on cooker hobs will have to be fitted with flame failure cut-out devices. Currently it is so easy for a gas ring to be blown out when the caravan door, or half the door, is open and the failure goes unnoticed as the gas continues to flow. Several caravan manufacturers have already anticipated this regulation and have the flame failure cut-outs installed. Others, so far, have not, and it is a point to look for when you are buying a new caravan.

The connection between the regulator on the gas cylinder and the caravan's gas supply system is simple. Small bore copper pipe, which feeds the gas appliances in the van, terminates in the gas cylinder storage locker with a brass fitting, which accepts a special neoprene tube as a gas tight push-fit. However, a small jubilee clip should always be used as a safety measure. A short length of this tubing goes to the regulator on whichever gas cylinder is in use.

The working pressures of butane and propane differ, so be sure to obtain the appropriate tube. Better still use tubing marked BS 3212, which covers both butane and propane.

It is also most important to use the correct type of regulator, depending on whether butane or propane is involved, because of this difference in working pressure between the two.

Switching from butane to propane for winter caravanning therefore means switching regulators also.

The neoprene tubing is purpose-made; it is available from caravan dealers, and only this tubing should be used. It does not last forever, and ideally should be replaced every year. Its cost is negligible. The year of manufacture is printed on it, and should you buy a secondhand caravan with old tubing – replace it. The regulator also will not last forever, and should be replaced after about four years.

It is worth mentioning here a problem raised in the April 1989 issue of *Practical Caravan*. Vans manufactured in Germany (in this instance a 'Burstner' van) use propane rather than butane. We know that this operates at a different pressure, and if one wishes to convert to butane in the UK, an appropriate regulator must be fitted. New jets may also be required on each appliance.

The regulator fitting to a Calor gas 7kg cylinder is a clip-on type, and on the smaller 10lb one it is threaded, so again, different types of cylinder require different regulators. Do note that these 10lb butane cylinders and regulators have left-hand threads. Don't waste energy trying to disconnect the regulator from an empty container when all you are doing is tightening it! Propane cylinders have right-hand threads.

A useful pressure gauge is available to fit between cylinder and regulator. This will tell you how much gas you have left, and will also serve to detect a leak in the gas system. You can, however, get a good idea of the amount of gas left by picking up the cylinder and comparing it with the other (full or empty) cylinder. Since the gas in the cylinder is in liquid form, sloshing it about will give you a good idea of the amount contained.

We know that gas powers your cooker, fridge, space heater and water heater if fitted. Additionally, many older caravans had gas lighting. Many caravanners preferred the homely hissing noise, softer light and warmth of a gas mantle to the harsher light of a fluorescent strip with its frequent radio interference.

The flue of many gas fridges is often vented into the awning, if rigged. For people sleeping in the awning this presents no problem, although there should be some ventilation in the awning.

There is no legal reason why a caravan may not be towed with a gas fridge alight and functioning, although it is not to be recommended. If you really must have your fridge working en route, use the 12-volt electric function of the fridge and run it off your car system via the 12S cable. It does consume a lot of current, however, and involves a special wiring job.

What you emphatically *must not do* is fill up with petrol on your journey while your fridge is functioning on gas. More than one disastrous forecourt explosion has occurred through petrol fumes being exploded by the flame of a gas fridge. This is more likely with a motor van due to the proximity of the fridge air inlet to the petrol pump. Safety regulations forbid any naked flame within 14 feet of a petrol pump. It is advisable to carry a few spare washers for the connection between the gas container and regulator – the washer here needs replacing fairly frequently. If you have a gas light in the van, carry a spare mantle or two. These should be stored where they will not receive knocks.

A final and useful tip about gas is, when exchanging an

empty cylinder for a full one, try not to be issued with an old or tatty looking cylinder. When containers have been in use for a length of time, a distillation of tarry liquor collects in the bottom of the cylinder. If the cylinder is used until completely empty, this gooey substance can clog your gas appliances. In the case of something like a gas water heater, this can mean an expensive stripping down and cleaning job. Go for a reasonably new looking cylinder, therefore, if you have the chance.

Checklist: Gas Supply

- Butane (blue cylinders) for everyday use. Propane (red cylinders) for winter or low-temperatures caravanning.

- On cylinders with threaded outlets, butane (blue) have left-hand threads, propane (red) have conventional right-hand threads.

- Replace the regulator unit after about four years. Annually replace the neoprene tube which connects the regulator to the caravan copper pipe system.

- For the UK only, Calor gas and Shell supply (butane and propane). On the continent, Camping Gaz (butane only). You need an adaptor to use a Calor gas regulator with a Camping Gaz container.

- Have the gas system pressure-checked during the annual service.

- If you install a gas appliance on a DIY basis, have it checked.

Chapter 9

Electricity Supply

Electricity (12-volt)

Before the advent of 220/240-volt mains in caravans the standard source of electricity was a 12-volt battery, and for many British caravanners it still is. European caravanners have had mains electricity for many years and to them it is standard equipment, although current consumption can be restricted to as little as 2–5 amps. (We will come back to mains supply shortly.)

The battery is either in the van, or you use the car battery, or both. One of the connections on the 7-pin electric socket(s) on the car towbar carries 12-volt power (suitably fused) from the car battery and you can plug the caravan lead into the car either directly alongside the van or wherever, to run lights etc.

On the basis that periodic use of the car recharges the car battery, whereas the caravan battery is steadily discharged, it is obviously better to plug into the car whenever possible and use the caravan battery as a standby when the car is away. You can charge your caravan battery in situ from the car when the outfit is on the move, or charge it in the car boot when the car only is being used. This needs the installation in the car of a special relay, which disconnects the caravan battery when it is not actually being charged and prevents current from the caravan battery feeding back into the car. Charging in the car boot is more effective, since when the battery is in the caravan, the longer wire runs plus 7-pin connections will all cause voltage drop, and a less effective charge is obtained. If you charge your caravan battery actually in the van, make sure it is in a separate, well ventilated locker, *not* in the gas cylinder locker. This is because a battery in the process of being charged gives off inflammable gases. We have seen that an amendment to the BS 4626 now makes it mandatory to store gas cylinders and the battery in separate compartments. There is no legal requirement, however, to modify older vans.

We always use the plug-into-the-car system whenever we can, and even without a mains hook-up we can have a 16-day holiday without exhausting the caravan battery. We have a 60 ampere hours battery, and with this plus use of the car battery whenever we can, we run a water pump, a radio/cassette player, an electronically governed gas water heater, an electrically flushed toilet and internal lights. (The small amount of current used by the Carver water heater can be virtually discounted.) We can be independent of mains electricity at all times, if needs be.

If you wish to install some electrical device such as an extra light or cassette player, go to a dealer and tell him what you want to do, and get the correct gauge wire. Don't use the thinnest cheapest wire you can get, 'because it's only 12 volts'. The resistance offered to a current passing through a wire is in inverse proportion to the thickness. Wire which is too thin will result in voltage drop or even a possible fire risk depending on the current consumed by the appliance.

There are, of course, other 12-volt appliances used in caravans in addition to the few we ourselves use. There are vacuum cleaners, fans, electric razors, hair dryers, etc, not to mention television. Fridges, as mentioned earlier, should only be used on 12-volt electricity when on the move and the power supplied by the car.

Herself has a small hair dryer and a pair of 12-volt curling tongs which both work off the cigar lighter socket on the car – the car therefore frequently doubles as a hatchback and a salon! (The hair dryer makes a good early morning de-froster in the winter.)

Your choice of battery for the caravan depends on the number of accessories you want to run, and the current they consume. The following is a short list of commonly used 12-volt caravan appliances and a guide to the current they use.

Appliance	Current (in amps)
Single strip light	0.7
Double strip light	1.3
Water pump (varies with pump rate of flow)	1.5–3

Appliance	Current (in amps)
TV (black and white)	2
TV (colour)	3
Fridge	8
Carver GE immersion heater	2.7

This table shows that a colour TV and a water pump capable of supplying a shower will make a fairly heavy demand on the caravan battery.

A new caravan will obviously be wired correctly and the circuits fused for the equipment that the caravan carries. If you have an older van, however, you may well want to install extra equipment, eg a radio/cassette player or water heater or perhaps a new battery. Any of these tasks would be simplified by asking the Caravan Club to send you their excellent leaflet *12-volt Installations in Trailer Caravans*. This leaflet covers in detail the choice of battery, the type and size, and also recharging and maintaining it. It gives help with installing and wiring extra appliances and advises on the correct gauge of wire, types of fuses, and so on. The Camping and Caravanning Club can also supply this type of technical advice.

Batteries can vary from a small car battery (about 30 ampere/hour capacity) to a jumbo size 90 ampere/hour. Before opting for the latter, consider the fact that it weighs about 60lbs! In basic terms the smaller the battery the sooner it will exhaust itself. Against this, the less current you can consume the longer the battery will last, regardless of its size. You may go for the option of recharging a small battery whenever you go out in your car, by connecting it up to the relay wired in the car boot. (Do ensure that the battery is firmly secured.) Our 60 ampere/hour battery is the Chloride 'Portapower' type and is designed to discharge slowly, unlike a car battery which faces spells of heavy demand from the starter motor. We have a simple two-way switch in the system enabling us to run off either the caravan or car battery. The van battery easily lasts a 16-day holiday without recharging, since we can plug into the car most of the time.

The Chloride battery will fit into an invaluable accessory called a 'Lab-Craft TP2' trailer pack. This consists of a well ventilated storage box which is wired to enable the battery to be recharged by the car either in the caravan, or in the car boot when only the car is moving, or from a mains electricity source. If the pack is used, no relay is necessary when charging from the car.

In addition to your in-van electrical gadgets you have the road running lights, side, tail, stop, number plate, indicators and – where fitted – high intensity rear fog light plus the new 'outline marker' lights. All these functions plus your domestic lights and appliances are powered from the car, when car and caravan are connected via either one or two 7-core umbilical cords and 7-pin plugs and sockets. The caravan half of these 7-core cables usually terminates at the front of the van inside one of the bed lockers, and there you will find your fuses. Make sure you know where to find and identify them, and be sure to carry some spares.

One 7-pin plug and cable used to suffice, but since the introduction of high intensity rear fog-lights, modern caravans need two connections, when legally required. This is because if your caravan is fitted with rear fog light(s) and your tow car was so fitted when new, then a connection for the fog lights must be available between the car and caravan.

The one plug only system supplied all the road lights plus internal van lights, accessories etc through what is known as a 12N plug (N for Normal). The second plug, where used, is called the 12S (Supplementary). 12N plugs (plastic) tend to be black whereas 12S are either grey or white. It is impossible to connect the wrong plug to the wrong socket. The connections are made via pins and tubes (male and female) and whichever connections are male on the 12N are female on the 12S and vice versa. Since the introduction of the two plug system, the separate functions of the individual wires have been rearranged between the two plugs. The pin which used to carry the wire for internal van lights etc in 12N plugs now carries the fog lamp, and internal lights and accessories are now pin No 4 in the 12S plug. Other 12S plug functions are items such as caravan battery charging and fridge operating on the move, if required. There is an earth pin and a pin for reversing lights; so far, the two remaining pins in the 12S plug are not allocated. On the 12S plug, terminal no 5, brown, can be used as a sensing device (warning lamp) thereby leaving only terminal 7 not allocated.

These plugs and sockets are not indestructible. Damp gets in inevitably and corrosion sets in, grub screws seize up and so on. They are not difficult to replace. New ones of both types are available from caravan dealers and motor accessory shops. With a new plug and socket you will get a wiring diagram; all the pins are numbered and all the wires are clearly colour coded.

Many failures of internal or road lights are due to faulty connections via corroded plugs, or bad earth connections on side lights, indicators and so on. They are simple to check, clean and tighten up.

Mains Electricity (220/240 volts)

Coming to the subject of mains (220/240-volt) electricity makes me stop and reflect a little. The earliest caravans were horse-drawn, illuminated by an oil lamp, and cooking was done over a wood fire by the roadside. We have progressed a long way since then, and I wonder where it will stop. My family have caravanned for over 20 years and we love it, with its implications of a slightly more basic way of life. We are all for lightweight chassis, insulated bodies, double glazed windows and yes, hot running water, but if we insisted on absolutely every modern convenience I think we would prefer to stay in an hotel. We can manage very nicely without television for starters. A fortnight free of the haunted fish tank is a blessed relief and we felt, until recently, that we could do equally well without mains voltage electrical appliances.

Our last caravan did not have mains electricity and rather than having it installed we invested some £75 in a transformer called a 'Ranger Power Pack'. (These are stocked by any good caravan dealer.) It converted on-site mains current – English or continental – into 12-volt direct current. We just plugged our caravan 12S plug into the compact 'Ranger' unit, instead of plugging into the car. (The unit has both 12S and 12N sockets.)

The transformer sat underneath the caravan, plugged into the site hook-up point, and gave us a constant 12 volt supply, as well as keeping the caravan battery constantly charged up. In fact with a 'Ranger' unit, one would not need to carry a caravan battery if always camping on sites with mains hook-ups.

Our present caravan came fitted for mains electricity, and on sites with mains hook-ups we use an electric kettle and also run the fridge on mains. Both these functions represent a significant saving of gas. In addition the on board mains powered battery charger gives us unlimited 12 volt current. Water pump for taps and shower, cassette player and lights can all be used without concern for 'nursing' the caravan battery. Our water heater is powered by gas only, but hopefully one day we shall have a dual powered gas/electric job, which will mean a further saving of gas.

We often use sites without mains electricity. Summer holidays are often spent on the Continent where there are indeed mains hook-ups on most sites, but two- or three-day breaks often find us in the corner of a remote field in Derbyshire or the Yorkshire Dales, with only basic facilities. Having said that, I notice that an increasing number of Certificated Locations and similar small sites are now being equipped with a few mains hook-up points.

So if you want mains electricity, it's there to be had. Only a very small number of new models are without it, and this has come about over a fairly short period of time. You do of course still have a sophisticated 12-volt system for lighting, water pump, the gas powered water heater, radio and so on. The mains circuit usually gives you two or three conventional flat 3-pin sockets for mains appliances, plus the invaluable facility for keeping the caravan battery fully charged.

The appliances used must be carefully considered for consumption, since on most UK sites with mains hook-ups, the maximum current you may consume at one time is from 10–16 amps. On non-club and continental sites it can be much less. If this is exceeded a circuit breaker operates and you and your neighbours are without power.

Don't take the 3kw kettle from home. A mains kettle used in a caravan should not be of a higher rating than 1000 watts. There are plenty of these available. Such a kettle would consume about four amps, and that might well prove to be about enough on some sites.

Kettle, toaster and fridge are examples of items which can usefully be used on mains electricity, and all reduce the consumption of gas which would otherwise be the fuel source. Television is another obvious mains user.

Mains electricity in a caravan is not without its snags. Incorrectly used or installed it can be lethal. British wiring regulations imposed on installations and the supply of current tend to be more exacting than their continental counterparts. For example, electricity supplied on British hook-up points has known polarity, that is, live current is supplied through the live or positive wire and it returns through the negative or neutral wire. For this reason British switches – which turn the appliance on and off – are single pole, which means that only the live wire is cut when switched off.

It is possible to hook up to some continental points and get the polarity reversed. This is particularly common on some French camp sites. What in fact is happening with 'reversed polarity' is that live or 'positive' current is supplied through the negative or 'neutral' wire, and is returned through the 'positive' wire. In other words the current is flowing the 'wrong way round'.

My first memorable experience of the French domestic electricity supply goes back about 30 years, when we used to stay in a delightful, homely, slightly primitive family hotel in Brittany.

There was one toilet per floor and it was lit by a 40 watt bulb. Some energy conscious character had cunningly wired this so that the brass bolt which secured the door completed the circuit and switched on the light. This ensured that it was impossible to leave the light on when leaving.

As French toilets go it wasn't bad, though no doubt it has now been modernised. It's probably got a 60 watt bulb and a low level cistern with one of those magic buttons which you lift in order to flush. Back in the late fifties however it still had the original cast iron, high level cistern. This was supported on ornate wrought iron brackets, and along the front, cast in relief, was the name of the originator, one Hercule Leclerc (1929).

For flushing purposes good old Hercule had supplied a generous length of elegant metal chain, and having completed the flushing process one day, I released the brass bolt on the door while still holding on to the chain. I promptly got 220 volts up one arm and down the other. Why operate the bolt while holding the chain? You may well ask. I don't know, I just did. I can tell you that you only do it once, it does tend to make the eyes water. Feeding current through a door bolt is bad enough; on top of this the circuit was doubtless earthed through the domestic water pipes, hence the current going to earth via the toilet chain and me.

We love France and the French people dearly; they have contributed much to civilised society as we know it, but domestic electrics is not one of their stronger points. It has been hinted that I seem to know more about eccentric sanitary facilities than caravanning, and that I would be better employed writing a book about memorable privvies. Maybe I will. For now, however, back to mains electricity.

We were discussing reversed polarity, where the current is incorrectly flowing into the appliances via the return wire, and returning via what should be the positive, or live wire. Using a British single-pole switch under these circumstances means only cutting one wire, but we should be cutting what is in effect the neutral wire. This means that live current is still flowing into the appliance, even though the switch is 'off', because the current is flowing and returning through the wrong wires.

If caravanning abroad, it is strongly recommended that you purchase from an accessory shop a simple and inexpensive gadget called a W4 mains tester. This plugs into one of your standard flat 3-pin mains sockets, and by means of three small neon lights it will warn you if you have reversed polarity, and most importantly it will warn you if you have no earth. I have on two occasions detected reversed polarity on continental sites, and corrected the situation very simply, as follows.

To cope with reversed polarity you need two or three feet of three core cable, the same gauge as the mains cable leading from the caravan to the hook up bollard. You also need an extra plug and socket for mains cables. These are both coloured blue and conform to BS 4343. On the other hand, you could chop off a couple of feet from your existing mains cable. Do this at the caravan end, the end which has the female socket attached. Replace this socket on the mains cable with your new socket, taking care that the three wires in the cable are fitted to the correct terminals on the socket. Your mains cable is now back as it was before, only a little shorter. You also have a two foot length of cable in addition, with a female socket at one end. You must now connect the new male plug to the other end of the short piece of wire, *but connect the live and neutral wires to the wrong terminals.* In other words, change the live and neutral wires over with each other. The earth wire (yellow/green) must of course *always* be connected to the earth terminal only.

If on hooking up to the camp site mains you find, via the W4 tester plug, that reversed polarity exists, disconnect the mains cable from the hook up bollard, then disconnect the mains cable from the caravan. You now insert your two foot length of 'changeover' cable between the caravan and the mains cable, and reconnect the mains cable to the camp supply point. The camp supply has reversed polarity, but by interposing your 'crossover' length of wire, the current enters the caravan correctly wired. This 'crossover' piece of wire and the W4 mains tester was referred to in a really first class article on mains electricity which appeared in the Camping and Caravanning Club's magazine during the summer of 1992. It was written by Ralph Lee, the Club's very knowledgeable (dare I say veteran?) technical officer. The article unveiled many of the mysteries of electrical lore in very easy to understand terms. I am indeed grateful to Ralph and to Peter Frost, the magazine's editor for allowing me to paraphrase some of this most informative feature.

The article likened the flow of electricity through wires to the flow of water through hose pipes. Imagine an electric cable attached to a simple apparatus, say a light bulb. The current flows though the live or positive wire, heats up the filament in the light bulb and returns through the neutral wire. Ralph draws a parallel between this and a simple water turbine driven by water pumped through a 'supply' hose pipe. The water drives the turbine, then returns to the reservoir through another 'return' pipe. If however, water was flowing to the turbine through the return pipe and returning via the supply pipe, you would, in electrical terms, have reversed polarity. We can carry this analogy a stage further, and consider an electrical 'Residual Current Device'. Suppose there were a leak in one of the hose pipes carrying water to or from our turbine, then water would be returning to the reservoir at a lower rate than that at which it was pumped out. If we had meters to detect the imbalance between the two rates of flow, we could then shut down the pump and prevent further leaks. That is exactly what a residual current device (RCD) does in an electrical installation. If current is leaking from the circuit and going anywhere other than where it is intended, then an RCD will cut off the current in milli-seconds. Caravans fitted for mains electricity are fitted with RCDs and also with fuses, or 'trips' which also break the circuit in the event of an overload of current, or a short circuit.

We spoke of a mains cable to enable you to connect your caravan with the nearest hook up bollard on the campsite. This should be obtained from a caravan dealer and will be supplied in the correct gauge wire, which is essential. It is recommended that a cable should be a minimum of 25 metres in length, and it will be fitted with BS 4343 blue plug and socket. It is worth noting that with the introduction of 1993 models, many caravan manufacturers are supplying a mains cable as standard equipment but in several cases these are less than the recommended 25 metres long.

I cannot over-emphasise the fact that installing or modifying mains electricity in a caravan should preferably not be tackled by an amateur, no matter how good his DIY achievements. If you wish to have mains power installed in your van you should get it done by someone authorised by the National Inspection Council for Electrical Installation Contracting (NICEIC), and obtain either a NICEIC inspection or comple-tion certificate signed by the inspector/contractor. There are many such people who advertise in the caravan magazines; at the time of writing the cost of such installations is around £150. If an engineer is not accredited to the NICEIC, don't hire him. (The Caravan Club have an up-to-date NICEIC list.)

Any new or secondhand caravan with mains power should be sold with an electrical inspection certificate, and any mains installation should be inspected annually for the sake of your own safety and that of your family.

Spare fuses should always be carried, and it is also a good idea to keep one each of the road light bulbs as spares. It is worth noting that in France it is mandatory to carry spare light bulbs for both car and caravan.

This is a complicated subject and I have only touched on it here. If you are going to invest in a van with mains electricity, or have it installed in an existing van, do read up the subject first. Ask the Caravan Club for their excellent explanatory leaflet called *Hooking up to Mains*, or ask for advice from the Technical Officer of the Camping and Caravanning Club.

The National Caravan Council publish *A Guide to Electrical Installations in Touring Caravans*. They have recently decided to withdraw this from general circulation, and make it available only to the trade, not the general public. Behind this move lies the conviction that installing mains electricity in a caravan is not a DIY job, and I would whole-heartedly endorse this view.

There are currently a number of accessory firms who advertise kits for installing mains electricity in vans, but as safety standards become ever more strict, these people may well find themselves having to withdraw this gear from sale. Repeat. Installing mains electricity is a job for a *professional*, and a qualified professional at that.

We ourselves used to think that mains electricity and touring caravans don't go together – we didn't like to think of all that rain water and all that electricity. Progress has overtaken us, however, and mains electricity is now the rule rather than the exception. Certainly if properly installed and properly serviced it is very safe and a great convenience. Probably we're just old-fashioned. Horse-drawn caravanners at heart!

Checklist: Electrics

- On 7-pin plugs and sockets joining car and caravan, keep all connections clean and free from corrosion.

- Keep all earth connections on the caravan body/chassis clean (commonest cause of malfunction of road lights).

- Use a proper caravan/boat-type battery in the van, not a standard car battery.

- Don't run your fridge off a 12-volt supply unless actually towing (on the move) – you'll flatten your car battery.

- Locate and familiarise yourself with the caravan fuse box.

- Keep a few appropriate spare fuses handy in the caravan.

- To install mains electricity in a caravan go to a member of NICEIC. Don't do it yourself.

- Use correct low-consumption mains appliances, or you will blow the camp-site circuit.

- Check the power available. Continental sites generally supply power at a lower amperage than the UK sites.

- If you're not familiar with 'RCD' and 'reverse polarity' (and who is?) do request information from one of the clubs. They will gladly send you a simple but comprehensive leaflet on mains electricity.

- Caravan mains are a little more involved than domestic mains. Don't take chances that would put the lives of your family at risk.

Chapter 10

Caravan Heating

Unless you are a strictly Mediterranean/fair weather only sort of caravanner, some kind of heating is essential. Even English summer evenings can be chilly. You can always warm up the van a little by lighting a couple of burners on the cooking hob, but this is scarcely efficient or economical, and it still leaves feet cold!

Gas is the most usual source of heating power, used in some sort of space heater. Heaters are not found as standard equipment in older caravans and we made reference on page 36, when discussing internal fittings, to the fact that older vans may have had a gas heater fitted, but with no external flue. These are indeed quite safe *provided* that adequate ventilation exists.

Modern caravans are nearly all equipped with some form of heating, usually a gas fired space heater fitted with an external flue. The smaller heaters are flued or vented through the caravan floor; larger capacity heaters have a small stove pipe, or chimney, which emerges through the roof.

There are a number of efficient systems made, but probably the one most commonly fitted as original equipment is that produced by Carver and Co.

Obviously caravan sizes vary considerably, and so must the output of a suitable heater. Carver's three models vary in heat output from the equivalent of 1.6 kW to a jumbo-sized 5.5 kW (with gas consumption varying in proportion). These space heaters are all (except the largest) vented under the van floor, and all feature a flame failure safety device where, in the event of the flame being extinguished, the gas supply is shut off.

These space heaters can be used by themselves as single units, but can also be the heat source for blown air central heating. Hot air from the heater is blown by a 12-volt electric fan through plastic pipe, or trunking, to all parts of the caravan. The installation and routeing of the trunking is best done before the caravan furniture is installed. It is complicated to install later and, therefore, somewhat expensive.

A part central heating kit is available, however, currently about £80 in cost, and this efficiently enables the DIY caravanner to pipe hot air around the feet of occupants sitting in the forward dining/sleeping area, also into the toilet compartment. (Believe me, that is really luxurious!) This hot blown air of course is in addition to the normal space heating function, which seems to retain its efficiency even when the blower is on. I have installed one of these part central heating hot air kits in our caravan. It runs off our Carver 1800 model space heater, and works very well.

Some larger caravans are fitted with a 'wet' central heating system, ie hot water is piped around the caravan to suitably positioned radiators, just as in a domestic central heating system. This calls for a fairly powerful gas heater to run it which is usually flued through the roof. A 'wet' central heating system is generally most efficient, but suffers from the drawback of taking rather longer to warm up than an instant space heater.

Having said this there is a very efficient 'wet' caravan central heating system made by Optimus, which is installed in larger caravans, and users of this system speak well of its efficiency. It is, of course, supplied as original equipment and is not a DIY job.

Details of the 'add on' blow air kits can be had from Carver, and they are happy to send out brochures of all their caravan equipment. (See Useful Addresses.)

Chapter 11

Caravan and Camping Sites

In the UK

A great variety of caravan sites exists throughout the UK, many accommodating both tents and caravans and there are a number of guide books available listing camp and caravan sites by county. A comprehensive guide to camping and caravanning sites in the UK is available from the AA; this is a most useful, good value publication.

The regional Tourist Information offices around the country can also give details of local caravan sites.

The question of choice of sites again emphasises the value of joining one or both of the caravanning clubs, who between them have literally thousands of sites which are only available to members.

The Forestry Commission have a network of about twenty sites, located in areas of outstanding scenery, ranging from the Scottish Highlands to Wales and the New Forest. These are sited to provide a wide variety of activities from pony trekking to bird watching, boating and water skiing. An attractive full-colour sites brochure can be had from their office in Edinburgh. (See Useful Addresses.)

There are also sites in the ten National Parks in England and Wales. These are all areas of outstanding natural beauty, and the ten area authorities can provide details of the location of sites within the Parks. (These area authorities are all listed in Useful Addresses.)

Most commercial sites are open from March until the end of October, although some are open all the year. Most are set in attractive scenery, and usually offer excellent facilities by way of toilet, washroom, shower blocks and mains electricity.

An increasing number of Caravan Club and Camping and Caravanning Club sites offer hook-ups to mains electricity. The sites are all under the management of the Clubs and there is a permanent warden on site. There are already hundreds of sites between the two clubs, and all may be booked in advance although advance booking is not always necessary.

The greatest appeal for many Club members lies in the truly vast network of certificated locations throughout the country. Most, though not all, are on farms, where members are always sure of a warm welcome. Each location is licensed by the Club, and is solely for the use of Club members. A certificated location or hideaway offers only basic facilities – a fresh water tap, a sewage disposal point and a dustbin. Many offer fresh milk, eggs etc, but that's about all. Peace and quiet are the main features, but it is quite possible to tuck oneself away on a certificated site and yet be close to the facilities of a large town or seaside resort. The owner of a certificated location is allowed a maximum of only five caravans on the site at any one time, so you won't suffer if you're allergic to crowds.

Information from the Clubs

The Caravan Club issues free to members every two years an updated directory of Club sites and certificated locations in the UK, with much invaluable information on the technical and legal implications of towing a caravan, plus a wealth of sound advice generally. Additionally the Club's magazine, *En Route*, frequently features articles on various Club sites and certificated locations. There is no shortage of information for the caravanner on the subject of sites, at home or abroad. The main problem is being torn between the desire to return to places you've enjoyed so much in the past and finding time to visit all the attractive places you have so far only read about.

The Camping and Caravanning Club has a similar network of sites and 'hideaways' available to its members. These are detailed in the Club's sites directory, and are updated as necessary in the Club monthly magazine.

Membership of one or both of the clubs opens up a very large network of sites and locations which are not available to non-members.

Caravanning Abroad

When we talk of caravanning abroad we are talking in most cases about Europe. Further afield than this means either a long sea voyage, which with a caravan is fairly expensive, or a road journey of many thousands of miles.

Many caravanners have toured in the UK for years with no help from either the caravanning clubs or the motoring organisations. Going 'foreign' is a rather different matter, and here I would strongly advise membership of one of the caravanning clubs. They have vast experience of the needs, the wrinkles and procedures involved in taking your van across the water. They can book your ferries and your sites, if you wish. They can arrange your holiday insurance, including 'get home' recovery in the event of breakdown or accident to either car, caravan or crew. They will supply you with your international camping carnet (more of which later). They can supply you with sites guides for almost every country in Europe, including those which were, at one time, behind the Iron Curtain. They really are the experts.

You will find further reference in Chapter 18 to the touring services, both home and abroad, offered by the Caravan Club and The Camping and Caravanning Club.

Most European sites offer mains hook-up and toilet facilities. Many have a camp provisions shop, and perhaps a takeaway cooked food service, a bar and a swimming pool. Some are a great deal more basic, and the various sites guides give a fairly accurate description of what you may expect to find.

The Caravan Club's two-volume European sites guide often gives details of sites, which are the result of reports from members who have visited the location already.

Touring in Europe offers a very wide variety of sites. Having found the coastal resort or location you want, you may well find that a site two or three miles inland is considerably cheaper and less crowded, and is well worth the short drive to the beach. Also don't be put off by sites with ratings of only one or two stars – they won't have a swimming pool, but the facilities are often very good value for money. Often the municipal sites, as distinct from privately owned ventures, can also be well run, quite adequate and represent keen value for money.

When on the road, driving on the right may need some concentration to begin with. Moving away from the kerb, turning left at junctions and overtaking also need particular care but one gets used to it quite quickly. The Caravan Club's Continental Sites Guide and Directory has a comprehensive section at the beginning of the book on international traffic signs. Many of these are common to our road signs in the UK, but do study them thoroughly before you go. Ignoring traffic signs in your host country may well involve you in an on-the-spot fine, and being a 'foreigner' is not usually an effective excuse. The Club's Sites Guide and Directory carries a wealth of information on motoring country by country, together with information on currency, weather, public holidays, obligatory documents and equipment for car and caravan, indeed every possible scrap of information you could need for travelling abroad. The Camping and Caravanning Club can supply you with similar information through their associated club, the RAC. One point on driving, petrol in Europe tends to be more expensive than at home, although diesel is often cheaper, especially in France.

Naturally, when travelling abroad, you need passports for every member of the party, although husband, wife and children can all be on one passport. Visas are not required in EC countries but are necessary in some Eastern European countries. A telephone call to the London Tourist Office or the Embassy of your chosen country will clarify any questions on visas.

Remember to take the registration document for your car. If it is not your own vehicle, eg a company car, you must have a letter authorising you to take the car abroad on holiday. A 'green card' (from the vehicle insurers) is not essential in EC countries but you are strongly advised to carry one, and do make sure that the insurers know that you are towing a caravan. This applies both at home and abroad.

Medical insurance can best be covered by whoever arranges your holiday insurance, but if visiting EC countries it is well worth obtaining a form E111 from your local Post Office. This enables you to take advantage of the subsidised health care in the host country. A Post Office leaflet gives you all the relevant information. Getting the form E111 is not a complicated bureaucratic process and is strongly recommended.

Another important document is a camping carnet. This is like a camper's passport and is available from either of the caravanning clubs. At a continental campsite, the site office will retain your carnet throughout your stay, rather than holding on to your passport which could make for difficulties when cashing cheques.

On the subject of finance abroad, travellers cheques in sterling are the best way to carry money. Easily changeable at banks or large shops abroad, they can be supplied by your bank. In addition, it is wise to have with you enough currency of the country of your destination plus those through which you intend to travel, to tide you over for a few days. Access and Visa cards are acceptable at literally thousands of facilities abroad and, finally, you could carry a book of Eurocheques. These cheques are made out in the local currency and are eventually debited to your bank account at the current rate of exchange. However, you must support the cheques with a Eurocheque card. Eurocheques and cards can be supplied by your bank. There is, of course, a small service charge for issuing travellers cheques, plus a service charge for using credit cards and Eurocheques in your holiday destination.

The point has been made elsewhere that all travel details can be arranged by either the Caravan Club Red Pennant service or the Camping and Caravanning Club's Carefree service (see Chapter 18). If all this sounds a bit involved, believe me, it isn't. The opportunities to see other countries, people and climates, to enjoy wide varieties of scenery and the (usually) quieter roads for travelling, all combine to make the simple paperwork more than worthwhile.

The whole Continent of Europe is just down the road. There are ferries sailing from ports all around the coasts of England, Wales and Scotland. These connect us with every part of Europe's coastline, stretching from Scandinavia in the North to Spain in the South and West, and of course, with Ireland.

When making plans to 'cross the water', don't forget either Northern Ireland or the Republic of Ireland. Don't be put off by the troubles which beset that beautiful country. Obviously the border counties are probably not the best place to holiday, but the Irish are peace-loving, hospitable and very friendly people, and both North and South have some indescribably lovely scenery, with miles of near-deserted roads. Where else but Ireland could you be sure of getting a pint of draught Guinness in almost any post office? I call that a very civilised way to live.

Go down to the south west, spend a week or so in the utter peace of the Ring of Kerry. You will remember the holiday for the rest of your days.

Finally, there will always be someone to help you find your way around when abroad; perhaps other English families who have already been there for some time and have all the local information sorted out. English caravanners who would merely exchange a cautious nod on a site in Cornwall tend to fall upon each other with joyful cries upon meeting on foreign soil. You should have no difficulty in recognising your fellow Brits abroad. The women wear bras, the men wear socks and the kids drop litter.

Checklist: Caravan sites

● Sites vary – either privately and commercially run, or run by or approved by the Caravan Club or the Camping and Caravanning Club.

● Commercial sites tend to be medium to large. Facilities are fairly good and include toilets, showers and a shop, and maybe a swimming pool, bar, club room, take-away, children's play room etc.

● Club sites or locations can be large with comprehensive facilities, or five-van only affairs with a tap and a dustbin.

● The larger the site the better the facilities generally, and of course the larger the crowds.

● Peace, quiet and comparative solitude means joining one of the Caravan Clubs. Five-van sites are for members only.

● Good sites exist also in National Parks and on Forestry Commission land.

● Going abroad? Get a European sites guide from one of the caravanning clubs, or the equivalent from the relevant country's Tourist Office. Arrange your ferries, insurance etc through either of the clubs or the AA or RAC.

● See that your family and pets behave as you would want others around you to behave. Remember that when abroad we are all British ambassadors.

Chapter 12

Caravan Catering

This chapter is not about to provide a list of recipes – there are already a number of very good books available on the subject of holiday cooking, plus a steady supply of recipes and suggestions in the caravan magazines. This is a short section containing just a few general hints on feeding the crew. Remember that Mum is on holiday too, and slaving over a hot stove is probably not what she had in mind.

The two main options here depend on whether or not you have an oven. We have had caravans with and without, and nowadays we go without; remember, an oven can weigh 30–40 lbs. Most long holidays are taken in the summer, and you are unlikely to be roasting joints, or making Yorkshire puddings or cakes. We firmly believe that for the extra cooking facility provided, an oven does not earn its keep in terms of the extra weight to be carried. There are frequent advertisements in the caravan magazines for ingenious cooking pans which do the work of an oven, when used on a gas ring.

There is no great difference between holiday catering in the UK and on the continent. Fresh salads, fruit, bread, meat, eggs, fish – usually all are readily available. Fish, and meat such as chops, can either be cooked on a gas ring or grilled. One thing is certain – it would be most unwise to take your chip pan with you. A chip pan in a caravan represents far too great a fire hazard – if the children want chips, go out and buy them.

Don't take all sorts of food that you can buy when you arrive, as the weight adds up alarmingly. Take dried foods rather than tinned – a great saving in weight. Many caravan dealers in fact sell quite a variety of dried foods, including vegetables. Dried packet soups are a good buy. Arrange meals that are simple and quick to cook, and don't overlook the versatile qualities of a pressure cooker.

Do have your favourite home accessories duplicated in the caravan's equipment. A chopping board, a really sharp knife, an egg whisk and a good carving/bread knife would be useful (sliced bread is not always available) and don't forget a bottle opener and corkscrew. Take with you your favourite pots of herbs – you don't want to buy these specially, they last too long. If you are going abroad, take Oxo cubes, Marmite, etc; such items are not so easy to find. Use tea bags; they're easier to dispose of. Get some good square plastic storage containers for sugar, tea, coffee, etc.

When on the move, stack all your food stores firmly in a stout cardboard box and wedge this firmly on the floor, preferably over the axle. As little weight as possible should be up in the eye-level lockers. Use these for lightweight, unspillable items such as tea towels, kitchen paper rolls, clingfilm, etc. When on the move make sure that your cups, plates and glasses, plastic or otherwise, are securely stowed and padded with tea towels, and also that cupboard door latches are secure and effective.

Be fairly flexible about your meals. Rigid routines are not for holidays (except where small children are involved). Don't make heavy demands on the cook; as I have said, *everyone* in the party is on holiday. Eating out could make a very welcome change.

Finally, a thought about microwave ovens. In theory they can be used in a caravan fitted with mains electricity but whether or not to do so really needs some careful consideration. In its April 1989 edition, the Caravan Club's magazine *En Route* gave an excellent review of the pros and cons and made some of the following points.

The power *output* of an oven, expressed in watts, is *not* the same as the actual power *consumed*. In some cases the latter is more than double the former, and almost any microwave operated on a campsite circuit where the load is restricted to 5 amps will certainly trip the installation's circuit breaker. New and recently updated Club sites will offer 16 amps per pitch, but other sites could offer less – maybe 10 amps or, on many continental sites, as little as 5 amps.

On continental sites the voltage is likely to be 220, rather than our 240 volts at home, and this could lower the microwave's performance to the point of making it virtually useless.

A simple formula for establishing how many watts may be consumed is that volts multiplied by amps equal watts. Therefore 240 volts × 10 amps equals 2400 watts. A continental circuit might be 220 volts × 5 amps, which equals 1100 watts. This is clearly quite a difference, and insufficient for most microwaves. Microwave ovens are not designed to be shaken about or subjected to vibration. Towing could actually damage the unit, and with some models could invalidate the warranty.

Finally, there is the matter of weight. Most models weigh around 50lbs or more – do you really need this extra burden?

These comments should be taken in context. We are discussing the advisability of taking with you the microwave from your kitchen, without checking its suitability for caravan use. Many upmarket caravans are now fitted with microwaves as standard equipment, and these are obviously suitable for the job, although the problem of lower voltage abroad will still apply.

In general, then, microwave ovens should not be taken on holiday without prior serious consideration. Check all the facts, and consider whether a good tin opener and a saucepan might be a better alternative!

Checklist: Catering

- Keep it simple.

- Have the right kitchen accessories in the caravan. You can't achieve much with a bent spoon and a blunt scout knife.

- Don't load up with food that you can obtain as easily and cheaply when you get there.

- *Don't* have a chip pan; it is an extreme fire risk.

- If your caravan doesn't already have an oven, don't bother. A fridge is much more important.

- Loose tea leaves are a nuisance in a caravan. Use tea bags.

- Don't expect anyone to devote the entire holiday simply to catering for your every gastronomic whim.

- When you can afford it, eat out. It's part of the holiday.

Chapter 13

General Hints

This is just a collection of small tips and suggestions to help you enjoy caravanning, and perhaps make life simpler. Old hands could doubtless double the list, but perhaps they will also be able to pick up the odd point that hadn't occurred to them before.

Soft Furnishings

Many a second-hand caravan can be greatly improved inside by some new curtains and/or loose covers. Our last caravan was bought new. We chose it because it had the features we wanted at the price we could afford, and it 'felt right', but it was spoilt by skimpy, dreary curtains. Herself tracked down some attractive material in the local market, and made up more generous curtains which transformed the interior appearance. Remember to treat your curtains and covers with a flame retardant spray – it is well worth the very small expense.

Good quality seat cushions are worth preserving, particularly where they are subjected to use by a rampage of children. It is surprising what can be dropped or spilt on seats during a fortnight. Washable loose covers are well worth either making or buying. There are always adverts for loose cover making services in the caravan magazines.

Protection from Insects

Returning to the subject of curtains, we have anti-mosquito nets over all our opening windows, including the skylight. Netting (again from the local market) is fastened over the window openings with 2-inch long strips of Velcro sewn to the net and the corresponding pieces stuck to the wall around the opening with Evo-stik. On hot summer nights when lighting is needed and the windows are open, these are invaluable. A more up-market modern caravan will most likely be fitted out with insect-screen blinds on all windows and roof vents. Even to buy these complete and fit them yourself is an expensive and tedious task. The net and velcro system is both economical and effective.

We also use a hanging curtain, consisting of 1-inch wide coloured strips of plastic, in the door opening. It is fixed by small hooks and screw eyes above the door, and it really does keep the flies out.

Ventilation

Talking of fresh air brings us to the subject of ventilators. On chilly evenings it is tempting to stuff odd socks and tea towels into the ventilators and work up a good old fug. Don't do it. The ventilators are essential for safety, particularly if you have a gas heater without an external flue or even a fridge working. Ventilators are set in the walls of the van – at the top and also at floor level – and they ensure an adequate supply of essential fresh air. Should you be unfortunate enough to have a gas leak, the ventilators will do much to disperse the gas which will accumulate at floor level. Inadequate ventilation could result in a literally lethal explosion.

Laundry

You will find that a length of clothes line and some pegs are useful on a summer holiday. The need to wash the odd 'smalls' and tea towels, or to dry swimsuits and towels, always arises. It is a simple matter to rig a temporary clothes line, perhaps between van and car or even in the awning. (On a sunny day an awning can work up quite a formidable temperature.)

Tyres

Before setting off always check your car and caravan tyre pressures. Check them when cold, not when you stop for

131

petrol. You should frequently examine your van tyres for sign of splitting or cuts – not only the treads, but also the side walls. Accidental 'kerbing' can damage a tyre to the point of considerable potential danger.

Unlike car tyres, the tyres on a caravan suffer very little tread wear, it is the tyre walls which gradually weaken and deteriorate. Unfortunately this often tends to go unnoticed.

We made the point, when discussing second-hand caravans, that the safe life of a caravan tyre is about five years. This is another point which often gets overlooked. We shall go further into the subject of tyre safety in Chapter 15 on Maintenance.

Wheel Nuts

Check also your van wheel-nuts for tightness; use a decent sized wheel brace, *not* the brace used for winding down the corner steadies. Better still, invest in a torque wrench, to ensure correct tightness without overtightening. This should be at a torque setting of about 60lbs/foot for nuts screwed onto wheel studs and 65lbs/foot for bolts which go through the wheel and screw into the brake drum. Incidents of caravans losing a wheel en route are by no means un-common. Extremely dangerous and potentially costly, this hazard can be safely guarded against by correct checking and tightening.

There is a valuable accessory on the market called 'Pozilok'. This is a tight fitting plastic device which fastens wheel nuts together in pairs and prevents them from loosening. Two of these are needed on each wheel and they don't interfere with the fitting of wheel trims. I have them fitted on both my caravan wheels and they seem to be very effective. They currently cost £5 per wheel, and are available from Harrier Designs. (See Useful Addresses).

Don't go in for wheel trims which are located by wheel bolts passing through the trim itself. They are incredibly fiddly to cope with.

Wheel Adaptor Plates

On the subject of caravan wheels, don't be tempted to buy a special plate which will adapt your car spare wheel to fit the caravan in the event of a puncture. The adapted wheel mounting will possibly make it difficult for the temporary wheel to fit inside the van wheel arch. The offset fitting can cause damage to the wheel bearing, and apart from this you would have not only unmatched tyres on the van axle but probably also odd wheel sizes, which certainly does not make for stability or therefore safety. In any case, if you are unfortunate enough to suffer a caravan puncture and fit the car spare wheel via an adaptor plate, the law of perverse possibilities says that you will get a puncture in one of the car wheels fairly soon.

Some new caravans do come equipped with a spare wheel but sadly it is still a small minority. When, oh when, will caravan manufacturers realise that most people would gladly pay for a spare wheel, as part of the outfit? What chance would a car dealer have of selling a car without a spare? Until that enlightened day dawns, buy a spare caravan wheel, appropriate to your van plus a good quality tyre – it's well worth the outlay.

Spare Wheel Storage

We said earlier that many modern vans have large lockers at the front, to contain gas cylinders plus spare wheel. This makes for a lot of extra nose-weight. Many such vans are on an AL-KO lightweight chassis, and AL-KO make an excellent spare wheel carrier which fits under the van just ahead or astern of the axle. This is an ideal location for the extra weight of a spare wheel. That's where ours goes and I thoroughly recommend this accessory. Admittedly it is a chore to have to grovel under the van with an airline when checking the spare tyre pressure, and there is occasionally the vague dread that some 'forecourt rally driver' is going to motor over one's legs while thus engaged. Speaking for myself, I have survived so far however, and still think it's the best answer to spare wheel stowage.

Positioning your Caravan

In Chapter 2 on siting your caravan, I mentioned positioning the outfit so that in a strong wind the awning is on the sheltered side of the caravan. Some shelter from wind can also be gained by positioning the van behind a wall or clump of bushes, but in this connection try to avoid parking actually underneath trees. Various species of tree can drip sticky substances on to caravan and awning which take a lot of removing; birds will most effectively do the same thing.

If you are holidaying on the west coast of Scotland for example, or indeed on many continental coast sites, there could well be quite a strong prevailing wind. Don't site your caravan so that you present the side of the van (opposite to the awning) square on to the wind. This will cause your caravan to rock about. Site your outfit about 45° away from the prevailing wind so that a corner of the caravan is presented to the wind, thus offering much less resistance.

When siting, consider also the path of the sun. Wind and other considerations permitting, you will want to see as much of the sun as possible; having set up your camp with awning rigged and pegged down all round, it is a bit depressing to find you would be much better off with the whole lot rotated through 90°! This advice goes for beaches also, particularly where there are cliffs behind or large rock formations. Because a particular resort or beach is on a south or west coast it doesn't follow that that is the way the beach will face. A beach on a peninsula or arm of a large bay can easily face north or east, even though it is on a south coast. A beach that's in shadow for most of the day is a bit disappointing after a long journey.

In-van Entertainment

If you prefer to listen to music in your caravan as opposed to watching television, do consider going a step further than a portable radio. Reception on portables inside a metal-clad van is not always ideal. Fitting a car cassette/radio unit with an internal aerial and stereo speakers is a simple task for the average DIY person. Overhead lockers, cupboards and/or shelves will house one of these very compact and neat units, and likewise the speakers. Do make sure you have a suitable in-line fuse in the supply wire from your terminal block in the caravan.

Car accessory shops sell an internal aerial which will fit neatly to the inside of a caravan window. Small and neat, it needs a 12 volt supply which powers a small amplifier. This boosts the signal received by the aerial.

We have one of these for our caravan radio, it avoids cutting holes in the van body for a car type aerial and provides really good reception. I can strongly recommend it.

Portable radios are often plagued at night by interference from the fluorescent strip-lights in the van. This can be cured by fitting strip-lights which are specially suppressed against radio interference; alternatively, an inexpensive suppressor kit is marketed by Lab Craft, available from caravan dealers.

On the subject of radio and TV, don't annoy your neighbours. Caravans and awnings are scarcely soundproof, and noise carries far at night. You should never allow your music, merry-making, dogs or children to annoy other people. This is one of the basic principles of the Caravan Code. Silence at night is a matter which is strictly observed, particularly on many continental sites.

Tool Kit

Always carry a tool kit, but don't go berserk since weight quickly adds up here. We always carry a hammer (for awning pegs), a medium and small blade screwdriver plus the same size Phillips screwdrivers, a hand drill and bits, some fine emery paper for electric contacts, pliers, wire strippers, spare lengths of wire, plus of course, suitable fuses. Also take insulating tape (good for water pipes or car hoses in emergencies), a Stanley knife, miniature hacksaw, a few screws and fastenings plus self-tapping screws, a spirit level and tape measure, a can of WD40 lubricating spray, a small pot of grease, a few rubber bands, a tube of Evo-stik and some strong twine. In addition to these, we carry spanners, wrench etc for basic car repairs, plus a tow rope and a set of jump leads. A wheel wrench and jack for the van are always carried. We have rarely needed any of this equipment, but are sure we would have done so if we hadn't actually had it with us. Sometimes in the timeless tranquillity of a summer holiday, and armed with these items, I will take some vital part of the caravan to pieces and then re-assemble it again – just for the hell of it. This is a pastime which Herself views with a disappointing lack of confidence, but at least it keeps me out of the pubs.

Portable Larder

Another useful piece of kit is a camping larder. This is virtually an oblong box, about 2½ feet high, 18 inches wide and about 12 inches deep. It is made of lightweight nylon fabric with net panels for ventilation and has three hardboard shelves. It folds down completely flat for stowage and weighs very little. In use, it hangs from nylon strings with an 'S' hook at the top, and we hang it in the awning. It will accommodate a fair quantity of salad stuff, fruit and vegetables; all things which are not heavy but take up a lot of cupboard space in the van, and which are better stored out in the fresh air. It has a zip fastening and is completely insect proof. It is available in most camping shops.

Record What You Will Need

Keep a notebook with a checklist of everything you need to take with you, and I mean *everything*. Don't classify anything as being so obvious that only a halfwit would forget to pack it – more than one seasoned caravanner has got halfway to Dover before a casual query from the better half has established that the spare wheel/suitcase/passports/loo are still at home on the driveway. It could be advantageous for one person to be specifically responsible for the list, which should include absolutely everything that isn't actually screwed down in the caravan. Sewing kit, torch, tools, awning, cooking gear, bedding, fly swat – if it's needed, great or small, it should be in the book. Only when you have been finely honed on the stone of bitter experience will you have compiled a list that includes *everything* you really need to take. By this time, however, you will find you are severely overweight so you must start to edit your list. (If things go as they normally do, you will then find that you won't use half the things you take, and that you have urgent need of the bits you left at home. All this of course adds to the bitter-sweet charm of the sport.) It is well worth thoroughly checking your list, even though it takes time to compile. It's no good, for example, saying 'we must bring a left-handed corkscrew next time' and promptly forgetting about it – put it on the list there and then. The Caravan Club have a checklist with extra space for you to add your own special items, and a good caravan dealer can supply a similar list.

Carpet Protection

A thought about your caravan carpet: with the inevitable spillages of food etc, which are almost impossible to avoid, it does tend to bear the brunt of stains in the catering area. The

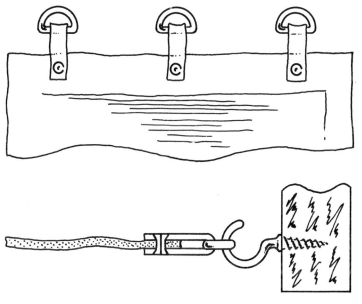

Carpet cover

answer is a length of clear, heavy plastic, carpet protector. This comes on a roll 27 inches wide and can be obtained from most accessory shops.

The trouble is that it 'walks' along the pile of the carpet, and should be secured as follows. Fix a short length of half an inch wide strong tape, or a strip of the clear plastic itself, at right angles to the edge of the plastic in three places, one towards each end and one in the centre. The tapes (or strips) should project about one inch beyond the edge of the plastic and finish with a small brass 'D' ring. Fasten the tape to the top of the plastic protecting strip, through the 'D' ring, and fold it back on itself to fasten underneath the strip. The tapes can be fastened to the plastic with either Evo-stik or pop-rivets plus washers, or better still, both. The 'D' rings then hook on to three small brass cuphooks fixed just above floor level at suitable intervals along the base of the kitchen unit. There is usually a stiffening batten running along the inside of the unit, and this will accept the cuphooks. The plastic can be sponged or scrubbed easily and will certainly preserve your carpet in this rather vulnerable area.

While actually working on the update for this edition of the book the value of this plastic carpet protector was vividly illustrated. We were holed up on a certificated location amid magnificent scenery in the Lake District. It was the Happy Hour. Wine had been poured and Herself was assembling a succulent omelette – mushrooms, tomatoes, onions, garlic, the whole works. The aroma in the confines of the caravan was at once tantalising and full of promise. At the crucial moment, armed with a spatula thing, Herself went to transfer the creation from pan to plate, and missed.

'Never mind,' you are thinking, 'at least it would fall on this much acclaimed piece of plastic.' Alas no. She missed that as well and once again waxed eloquent. Still, it's an ill wind; the dog thought it was her birthday, and we ate a little later. What we need now is either a bigger piece of carpet protector or bigger plates.

Inflatable Jack

A final thought on punctures. Actually getting a mechanical jack under the axle of a laden van involves a fair bit of low-level grovelling. The task can be made much easier with an 'Easylift' air jack. This is a sturdy inflatable airbag to which is connected a hose which fits over the car exhaust. With the engine running the bag inflates quickly.

The airjack comes in various sizes and cuts out all the backache of jacking. Available from New Concept (see Useful Addresses) and for use with car or caravan, model EL 01 gives an 18-inch lift. Remember, *never* go underneath the van when it is jacked up, no matter what the type of jack; use axle stands.

Checklist: General hints

- Brighten your caravan with new curtains/loose covers.

- Mosquito nets are a must in Europe (and in Scotland!).

- *Never* block up ventilators.

- Check tyres *and* wheel nuts.

- Do carry a spare wheel, plus jack and wheel brace.

- Avoid parking directly under trees.

- Install a car cassette/radio player – better than a portable one.

- Carry a tool kit.

- Keep a notebook or checklist of things to pack.

Chapter 14

Security

Thefts of caravans are increasing alarmingly and obviously it is a profitable area for those engaged in this nefarious trade. The problem for the van owner is twofold: first, to avoid having his caravan stolen in the first place, and second, to be able to positively identify it or enable the police to do so when and if it is recovered.

Immobilisation

The first problem is dealt with by making the caravan immobile on site. Originally this was dealt with simply by fitting a padlocked hitch lock. Locks are available to fit most

The Keep-It hitch lock.
Photo courtesy of Grove Products (Caravan Accessories Ltd).

types of coupling head, making it impossible to attach the caravan to a towing vehicle. However, bolt cutters will deal with most padlocks and determined caravan thieves will, if necessary, unbolt the entire coupling and jockey wheel housing from the 'A' frame, and fit another. All the caravan owner is then left with is his coupling head unit, complete with hitch lock still attached. Practised thieves have more than once stolen a hitchlocked caravan by fastening the coupling head (and hitchlock) to the getaway vehicle with rope, and removed the hitchlock at their leisure. However, hitch locks are a deterrent and will often prevent the spur of the moment theft where the thieves do not have time on their side; for example, caravan thefts from motorway service area car parks are by no means uncommon – it takes about 45 seconds for your caravan to be unhitched from your car, dropped on to the getaway vehicle and driven away. If you are making a stop at such a location it is really worth just dropping your jockey wheel, unhitching your van, applying the handbrake and fixing a padlocked hitch block. It only takes a minute or so.

Once established on a site, there are a number of precautions you can take to ensure that your caravan is still there when you get back from the beach. Hitch locks have already been mentioned; another practical deterrent is a pair of special corner steadies which, when lowered, can be locked into position making it impossible to raise them. One of the best devices is a dummy wheel. This is a steel plate which you bolt on to the wheel studs, having removed a wheel. It has a straight edge which rests on the ground, keeping the caravan axle at the correct height above ground level. If it is attached with special lockable wheel nuts (available from any car accessory shop) you will have given the thieves quite a problem. Of course you would remove your spare wheel from its carrier under the caravan. (Keep both the spare, and the wheel you have removed in the boot of the car.)

Probably the most thiefproof and reliable way of immobilising your van is with a 'Wheelok'. This is a virtually burglar-proof, lockable wheel clamp and is made by the firm who manufacture wheel clamps for the police. Priced at between £60 and £70, it is quite expensive but is about the

S.A.S. Wheelclamp.
Photo courtesy of Safe and Secure Products.

best device available, and well worth the cost. Available from caravan dealers, or in case of difficulty, contact Lionweld Kennedy Ltd. (see Useful Addresses).

A rigged awning, incidentally, is no deterrent to the quick removal of a caravan. A sharp knife run around the awning close to its joint with the van, and your awning is removed (and totally ruined) in seconds.

Identification

Now, should you lose your caravan, could you identify it? One 14-ft 1993 Superdream Spacegobbler MK II looks very much like another, unless you have added an extra coloured side-stripe or similar visible feature.

Keep a careful note of your caravan chassis number, although it is no problem to remove the identity plate from the chassis and substitute a forgery. (From 1987 caravans should have the number die stamped on the actual chassis, rather than on a separate plate.)

Note *any* internal modifications you make – an extra shelf, a different light switch, different curtains – anything that might identify the caravan. Use an 'invisible pen' to mark your chassis number or home post code on several surfaces: inside a cupboard door, under a bedding locker lid, etc. These pens are easily available and the writing only becomes visible under ultra-violet light. Get under the caravan and scratch the chassis number on the underside of the floor. Finally, etch the chassis number on all the windows. If you insure your van through the Caravan Club 5 C's Policy, they require you to do this; the Club will provide, at modest cost, a small kit to do the job.

Help from the Caravan Club

Another good reason for Caravan Club membership is that the Club maintains a computerised security register, listed by make, model, year, chassis number, etc, of those members who send in their caravan details. This started as a register of caravans insured by the Club but was soon extended to cover all interested members. In addition the Club maintains a register of all reported stolen caravans, as does the National Caravan Council (see Useful Addresses).

Regional police forces are making increasing use of these records, and the information has enabled many stolen caravans to be restored to their rightful owners. Caravan dealers are also contacting the Club when offered a caravan for sale which appears to be suspect, as a result of which doubtful deals have been nipped in the bud.

Locks and Alarms

So much for not losing the caravan. What about its contents? It is not necessary to get inside a van to steal it, as the thieves can always get inside once they have removed it from your location. The security of its contents on site is a different problem, however. The door lock is no problem to the person equipped for the job. There are only just over 100 different British door lock combinations, and any caravan centre can supply any key. Armed with these one would have access to almost any caravan in the country.

Additional door security can be provided by fitting a

S.A.S. High security replacement door lock.
Photo courtesy of Safe and Secure Products.

modified cylinder to the existing caravan door lock. These
are available quite reasonably from Safe and Secure Products
(see Useful Addresses). There are over 50,000 different
combinations of keys to these easily-fitted cylinders – well
worth installing.

Such a modification won't keep out anyone who sets about
the lower half of the door with a lever or jemmy, but you can
deter this character by fitting to the lower door a sturdy
deadlock which actually bolts through into the door frame
when locked.

This leaves the windows, which usually have three fastenings each. When leaving the caravan unattended, do
fasten all windows properly. This will deter the opportunist
thief, but you cannot keep out one who is really determined
to get in. At the expense of smashing the fastenings and
probably the window itself, anyone with a jemmy or similar tool can open a caravan window and, working on the
window inside an awning, would be unobserved even on a
busy site. In this case you must consider some sort of
electronic burglar alarm with a noise warning. Beware of

145

anything too sensitive, such as those designed to detect movement. A window trembler switch is easily set off just by the wind gently rocking the caravan.

Safe & Secure Products also market a caravan security system, incorporating both an internal and external alarm. They also produce the SAS wheelclamp, which is a pretty sturdy item. Details of all their security devices, including the caravan door locks, can be had from their head office in Bristol (see Useful Addresses). Details of your nearest stockists are available, or you may buy direct on a mail order basis.

Hitch locks, lockable corner steadies, dummy wheel plates and various types of burglar alarm are all well advertised in specialist caravan magazines, and as always a good caravan dealer will offer goods and advice.

It is not my intention to deter you with this dismal survey of possibilities. Thankfully, in twenty five-odd years, we have never had *anything* stolen. Caravans *are* ransacked however, and increasingly taken by theft. The moral is: do take reasonable precautions and don't cut corners with questionable insurance cover. Get your caravan and *all* its contents, including money, cameras etc, fully covered by a reputable insurer.

Caravan Registration and Identification Scheme (CRIS)

The previous few paragraphs have dealt with various wise precautions to do with giving your caravan an identity, by etching your chassis number or post code on the windows, and then registering your caravan with the Caravan Club.

All this has now been taken care of automatically, if you happen to be the proud owner of a caravan manufactured during or after 1992. The National Caravan Council, after much research and liaison work with every British caravan manufacturer, has come up with something we have needed for many years. This is the Caravan Registration and Identity Scheme – CRIS for short.

Every caravan made in Britain in the 1992 manufacturing year, and subsequently, will have an identity number unique to that caravan. It will be made up of letters and digits, and will be clearly die-stamped on the chassis and etched on the windows. The first part of the Vehicle Identity Number – or VIN – will identify, through the coded characters, the country of origin, then the name of the manufacturer, then single or twin axle. The next two characters will be a National Caravan Council identification, followed by the model year. The final part of the VIN will be the manufacture's own serial number for that particular caravan (as practised prior to 1992).

A new caravan will therefore be delivered to the dealer with the VIN already stamped and etched on, and the paper-work will include a registration document bearing the VIN and details of the caravan. Following the sale, the caravan dealer will fill in the buyer's details and forward the document to the National Caravan Council's central computer. The identity of both caravan and owner are then entered into the computer, in just the same way as motor vehicles and owners are recorded by the DVLC in Swansea. The registration document is then forwarded to the registered owner for safe keeping. (NOT IN THE CARAVAN).

Insurance

This section on caravan insurance is an important part of the whole subject of security.

As with household, car, personal or any other type of insurance cover, it is wise to get several quotes, look at the small print and thoroughly understand what you are getting for your money. It does not follow that the cheapest cover is the best buy, nor for that matter, that the most expensive is necessarily the best.

Many insurance companies and brokers will quote you for insurance cover on your caravan, but in this area it is probably sensible to deal with a specialist company.

Few people are better placed to fully understand the risks, and the probability of these risks actually happening, than the two caravanning clubs. Mention of their respective insurance services is made in Chapter 18.

Both clubs offer comprehensive forms of cover against the various caravan related disasters to which we are all exposed. The Camping and Caravanning Club actually offers £100 worth of free cover on camping or caravanning equipment and personal possessions while at home, en route to or from a camp site or while on a camp site in the UK. This cover automatically applies to a full member, and children under 17, and is applicable only during a current period of membership. Items in excess of £100 in value can be covered separately, and the Club can quote favourable rates for insurance cover on caravans, cars, motor caravans and houses. Full details are available from the Camping and Caravanning Club. (See Useful Addresses.)

We have mentioned earlier in this chapter the Caravan Club's register of members' caravans by make, chassis number etc. This is an important feature of the Club's service, and of course they offer practical forms of caravan insurance, the premiums varying with the value insured and the extent of the cover required. The Club can also quote for car, motor caravan and house insurance, as do the Camping and Caravanning Club. Two additional services offered by the Caravan Club are a pet care policy and insurance for small craft – sailing dinghies and similar craft.

We said earlier that specialists such as the two clubs are probably among the best sources of caravan cover, but there are a few companies who also offer specialist policies. Among these is the Olympic caravan policy, which offers four different levels of cover with a comparative scale of premiums. This is a good package, and is available through the Mobile Homes Insurance Service. (See Useful Addresses.)

It is important to realise that no insurance company will pay out on a claim for theft or similar loss unless the policy-holder has taken reasonable care of the property. Leaving a caravan unattended and unlocked, or with windows unfastened, or indeed without some form of anti-theft device on the van itself, would almost certainly be considered negligence on the part of the insured. On my own policy, I earn a 10 per cent discount on the premium by undertaking always to fit an approved wheel clamp when not actually towing. That is not the only anti-theft device we use by any means, but this type of requirement by the insurers is the sort of thing often found in the small print of a policy, so before opting for any sort of cover, do make sure you know what you are getting, and what you have to do to make sure you are covered at all times.

Checklist: Security

- Security precautions: two aims – prevent loss of entire caravan, and prevent entry and loss of contents.

- Preventing forced entry is virtually impossible but deterrents are well worth while.

- Preventing theft of the van means immobilising it by one, or preferably more, means.

- Immobilisation is essential during storage or lay-up.

- Etch your chassis number or postcode on caravan windows.

- Similarly, mark interior surfaces with invisible (ultra-violet) pen.

- Register your van's identity with the Caravan Club.

- A record of all stolen vans is maintained by the National Caravan Council.

- Take out a fully comprehensive insurance policy.

- Lock your caravan and car, whenever you leave them, even for brief absences. Your insurance will not cover you if you have not taken reasonable care.

- If you have a new caravan, *don't* keep the registration and identification document in the van.

Chapter 15

Maintenance and Laying Up

Most caravanners use their van from the spring through until autumn, then lay it up for the winter.

Many of the small jobs listed here can be done prior to laying up, or on recommissioning in the spring, or preferably check over on both occasions. Obviously a caravan is better stored under cover, bearing in mind that wet and damp are the main enemies. If under cover, however, adequate ventilation is essential. A caravan, like a car, will suffer more harm than good if it is shut in an unventilated, damp garage.

Tyres and Chassis

Starting at the bottom: check your tyres for damage – if you can jack up your van so that the wheels are off the ground, so much the better. Support the suspension or chassis on axle stands – don't let the weight rest solely on the corner steadies; they are not designed for this. If you cannot raise the wheels, then occasionally jack up, and partly rotate each wheel, so that the tyres are not constantly flexed in one position. The wheels would be better off removed from the caravan during the winter and stored in the garage, for two reasons. One, the tyres will benefit from not being flexed in one position; and two, it is not easy to steal a caravan without wheels.

Another timely warning on tyres comes from the National Tyre Distributors Association (NTDA). It appears that some older caravans with wheels designed for tyres with inner tubes have been fitted with tubeless tyres. This is a potentially dangerous situation which can lead to the deflation of tyres on cornering and even to the complete loss of the tyre from the wheel. The NTDA advise that wheels designed for tubed tyres should never be fitted with tubeless tyres and wheels designed for tubeless tyres should never be fitted with tubed tyres.

WHAT IS A SAFETY WHEEL?

A true safety wheel can perform the following -

- Lock the tyre onto the rim after deflation, even during a blow-out, by covering the well.
- Prevent flailing and premature tyre break-up - the cause of wheelbox damage.
- Provide limited run-flat performance whilst maintaining stability and control.
- Sandwich a section of rubber between the rim and road even while running flat.
- Protect the wheel rim from damage.

The safety wheel has a tough job to perform and Tyron does this well........on cars, caravans or light commercial vehicles..........for genuine peace of mind whilst towing or motoring.

NO STANDARD WHEEL CAN PROVIDE ANY OF THESE SAFETY FEATURES - WHETHER BRAND NEW OR AN OLD DESIGN.....Not even the standard 'safe' ones sometimes called Safety Wheels, for marketing purposes.

WHY THE MODERN WHEEL CANNOT BE A 'SAFETY WHEEL'

Caravan or car wheels, usually identical in design, are 'safe', when properly inflated, or they wouldn't be in general use. However, potentially dangerous problems follow tyre deflation, due to the fact that wheels have a well inside. They have to have a well, without it a tyre cannot be fitted or removed, so it's a necessary feature.

Bead retention devices (usually small humps) on most wheels are designed to help hold tyres in place, but are after ineffective once the tyre is flat. Think about it - to fit a tyre its beads are pushed over these humps. If large enough to hold the tyre in place after deflation, the humps would be too big for the beads to be pushed over in the first place!

WHAT HAPPENS AFTER TYRE DEFLATION

DEFLATED TYRE WITHOUT TYRON

If air is lost from a tyre it can move from its seating into the smaller diameter well, resulting in flailing and reduced control.

With the tyre able to slip over any 'humps' and into the well it's free to move up and down, side to side and around the rim. Braking becomes ineffective, with less tyre to rim grip as it runs on the smaller well diameter. Steering, cornering control and stability will be reduced and tyre flail can damage wheelboxes.

Running on a flat tyre will damage the rim and it can dig into the road, sliding or even turning the vehicle over.

Tyron fits inside caravan or car wheels to cover the well. If a tyre deflates, it has a platform to run on, and is firmly locked onto the rim preventing flailing and instability. Rubber is sandwiched between the rim and road, helping you stay in control.

Tyron gives limited run-flat capability helping maintain stability, steering and braking control while you drive on a flat tyre, for a short distance to a safe place to change the wheel. This isn't safely possible with any standard wheel.

Accident risk is reduced and even at speed you will have a greater degree of control to bring your outfit safely to a stop, after tyre deflation.

Tyron does not affect wheel balance and can be removed for tyre repairs by any tyre fitter, using the tool supplied.

DEFLATED TYRE WITH TYRON

POLICE & SECURITY APPROVED

Tyron is fitted on UK and Worldwide police, security, government and military vehicles and by UK and continental caravan manufacturers. It is approved by motor manufacturers (used with sucess on the RAC Rally) and has German TUV approval, all their testing proving Tyron increases the safety performance of any modern wheel - even on high performance vehicles.

NEW FOR 1992 - A new band, lighter yet even tougher, coping with the highest speed blow-outs and finished in a corrosion resistant material, meeting the requirements of Ministry of Defence STAN 03-11/2 Class 1 and BS3189:1973 Type 1A, with new precision manufacturing processes and procedures supplied within the scope of BS5750 Part 2.
ALL FOR THE SAME PRICE AS LAST YEAR - THE 4TH YEAR WITHOUT A PRICE INCREASE.

SEE Tyron **IN ACTION.**

CALL IN AND ASK TO VIEW THE TYRON DEMONSTRATION VIDEO AT MOST CARAVAN DEALERSHIPS (OR EVEN BORROW ONE FROM ANY TYRESERVICES DEPOT OR SPRITE DEALER).

Tyron is a registered trademark - Patented worldwide.

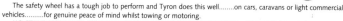

Owners of older vans may well be unaware of the actions of a previous owner with regard to replacement tyres, and after buying a second-hand caravan, owners are strongly advised to get the wheels and tyres carefully checked at a specialist tyre depot.

When a replacement tyre is wanted for a caravan, be it for the spare or straight on to the axle, one does not usually take the caravan to the tyre depot, just the wheel. It is all too common on these occasions for the owner to ask for a cheap tyre to be fitted, without mentioning that it is to go on a caravan. Whether it is a remould or a low grade tyre is not thought important. 'It will have a decent tread on it and that's what matters.' WRONG! There is far more to a tyre than just a good tread. For a start, on a single axle van – and this is the vast majority – each wheel is bearing about twice the load that each of the four tyres carries on an average car.

You should always specify that the tyre is for a caravan, and the depot should, if they are doing their job, fit a 6 ply or a reinforced tyre. If you examine a new tyre carefully you will see on the tyre wall a whole jumble of letters and codes, which almost need a separate handbook to interpret. You should find however the maximum load that the tyre is designed to carry and the maximum speed at which that load can be carried. A four ply tyre, a remould or any sort of 'bargain' tyre will certainly not come up to the specification you need.

Apart from being a security measure, removing the van wheels in winter will help preserve your tyres. An inflated tyre has its walls stretched, that much is obvious. In cold weather, with the tyre constantly flexed in one position, hair-line cracks or 'crazing' will take place on the walls, and to a lesser extent, even with the wheels jacked up. Better to remove the wheels and store them in the garage, loft or whatever, and deflate them. I know it means taking them to the garage to re-inflate them in the spring, but they will last longer, and they're worth some care.

My wheels come indoors and the van rests on two excellent lightweight high tensile alloy stands which bolt on to the brake drums, using the original wheel studs or bolts. They are not therefore strictly axle stands. They fold up when not in use, take up little space, and are very reasonably priced.

Called *Vanguard* stands, they are available, mail order, from J K Products, in Rawtenstall, Lancs. (See Useful Addresses.)

If you do not have a modern galvanised chassis, check for rust – any rust spots should be cleaned with a stiff wire brush and treated with a rust inhibitor. Halfords offer a variety of these. Paint over the area with black bitumastic paint, or better still use Finnegan's Hammerite in black. If any part of the chassis, suspension or brake mechanism shows signs of rust, treat as above then spray the whole lot with Finnegan's Waxoyl. (Again this is available from Halfords, and includes a hand spray applicator.) Waxoyl will inhibit rust, lubricate and form a hard wax seal against further damp. Care must be taken not to spray it on polystyrene sheeting which is often found as under-floor insulation. A chemical in Waxoyl will dissolve polystyrene, but is not harmful to wood or tyres.

Floors

Check the floor timbers for rot using a sharp, pointed knife. Any timberwork with rot requires immediate replacement. This could present no simple task, but is essential because rot in timber will soon spread. Floor timbers may be treated annually with a preservative such as Cuprinol; check with the caravan manufacturer, as the floor may already have been permanently treated.

For your own safety any work under a caravan must be done with it safely supported on stout axle stands. Don't rely on corner steadies, car jacks, stacks of rocks or bricks.

Gas and Water Pipes

While underneath, check gas and water pipes. Joints in gas pipes can be checked for leaks as follows. Turn on the gas at the relevant cylinder, ensuring that the gas taps at all appliances are in the off position. Brush a soap or detergent solution over the joints in the supply line. Any sign of bubbles will indicate a leak, and the gentle tightening of the nut with a spanner should effect a cure. If not, undo the nut from the joint, and replace the olive. The olive is a soft metal collar which fits around the supply pipe, and the action of tightening the nut will compress the olive against a recess in the joint, forming a gas-tight seal. Gas pipe joints and olives are readily obtainable from dealers, but make sure you get the correct size since more than one diameter of pipe is used on a supply system.

Fresh water pipes should be free from algae or blobs of discoloration. If the pipes don't appear to be clean, pump a purifying solution through the whole system and allow it to stand for a few hours before flushing through with clean water. Modern caravans are fitted with coloured rather than clear water pipes – black or blue for cold water, red for hot. This is partly because algae forms more readily in clear pipes. If your piping is badly affected by algae, replace it with non-clear piping. If you are doing some DIY plumbing, *do use* special red pipe for hot water, it is designed for the job.

You can obtain sterilizing tablets from accessory shops, or a preparation of sodium metabisulphite which is available from Boots or any wine-making shop (it is used extensively to sterilize wine and beer making equipment.) Check all water pipe joints for leaks, tightening up the jubilee clips if necessary. Before doing so, give the jubilee clip screws a squirt of WD40 lubricant.

Grease and Lubricate

Take a grease gun to the nipples on the drawbar around the coupling head mechanism. If the drawbar is covered by a plastic fairing, the nipples will be found under holes in the fairing. Ensure that the plunger attached to the coupling is free to slide in and out. This is usually covered by a flexible gaiter which should be free from cracks or splits. If it is split, replace it. Check that the inside of the coupling which fits over the towball on the car is adequately greased, the catch which locks the coupling on to the ball is lubricated, and its spring is effective.

Finally, lubricate the handbrake mechanism and both the axle of the jockey wheel and the winding handle. Wind the jockey wheel right down until the threaded stem drops out of its outer tube, and grease the stem before replacing.

Replace Damaged Seals

On the body of the caravan, check all seams and joints in the aluminium cladding, particularly at the corners of the van and around the skylight. Any mastic sealant which has dried and cracked should be cleaned out with a knife, and a non-hardening, special seam-dresser sealer should be forced in to replace it. This is rather a chore but very necessary. Ideally, all bodywork seams should be scraped clear of dried or flaking filler and be resealed with the correct mastic every three or four years. Your local caravan dealer can do this job for you, or supply you with suitable filler so that you can do it yourself. Few jobs will prolong the life of your caravan more than this important precaution. Until the arrival of bonded construction, caravans were made on a timber framework, the exterior and interior cladding then being added. If water gets at the timber frame the wood will rot, and the value of your caravan will decrease considerably. Replacement of rotting frame sections is an expert and costly business, and prevention is vastly preferable to the need to cure.

Clean Bodywork

At the end of a season the caravan could look rather travel-stained, dead insects and black streaks being the main features. A good wash in mild detergent followed by a hose down should cope with the insects. Use a stepladder and floor mop to deal with the roof. If washing does not move the black streaks, which usually appear under the windows, don't rush in with patent car cleaners. Car paint is usually cellulose while caravan paint is acrylic, and not all preparations are suitable for both. Some car cleaners tend to be mildly abrasive and can ruin the paintwork on a van. Personally I use a special creamy caravan cleaner called 'Silky', readily available from dealers. This shifts almost any marks and leaves an excellent gloss finish.

Check Lighting

All road lights on the caravan should be checked. If the washing has left moisture inside the plastic light covers, check the tightness of the holding screws and, if necessary, replace the rubber seals around the lights. Tighten up the screws inside the light fittings, ensuring that an adequate earth connection is made. A small squirt of WD40 in the bulb fittings is worthwhile. At the same time check your 12N and 12S plugs which make the electrical connections between caravan and car and if they are corroded, replace them. (This was covered in the 12 volt section, Chapter 9.) If they are in good condition, treat both, and the sockets on the car, with WD40 lubricant.

Clean and Ventilate Interior

Inside the caravan, ensure that carpets and cushions are cleaned, preferably vacuumed. Stand seat-cushions/mattresses up on edge to ensure a flow of air around them; better still, if you have space available take all movable upholstery indoors for the winter. If materials are left in the van, then use a small dehumidifier (available from any good DIY store) to gather any moisture. The Sellotape people market a good dehumidifier.

Drain Containers

If you leave your water containers and chemical toilet in the caravan, make sure that all are empty and dry. Leave off or open all screw tops, caps, valves etc, to ensure an adequate fresh air supply. Check all internal water and gas pipe joints for leaks. Remember that a water heater, either storage or instantaneous type, *must* be drained against frost damage.

Inner Surfaces

Thoroughly clean out and wash all cupboards and drawers, taking care that no crumbs are left about. (We had a resident mouse during one winter, which had gained access through a slightly oversized hole in the floor designed to take a water pipe. It must have had a rugged digestive system, for it ate everything it could find – wood, plastic and fabric!) Believe me, God's little furry creatures you don't need, so don't leave anything to tempt them, and don't leave access for them.

All metal hinges and catches on cupboards and work-tops should have a squirt of WD40.

We find the plastic edging strips around work tops and cupboard doors constantly peel off regardless of the quality of the van. A hot iron will often be successful in refixing them (this is how they were stuck on in the first place) or, better still, refit them with Evo-stik. If they have become bent or distorted, your local DIY shop can usually sell you something to match reasonably closely, as a replacement.

Professional Electricity Check and Service

Finally, if your caravan is fitted with mains electricity remember that the system should be checked professionally every twelve months, and a certificate issued. Don't overlook this. All these routine checks and tasks can, of course, be carried out for you by your caravan dealer – preferably one who is a member of the special Service Scheme organised jointly by the Caravan Club, the National Caravan Council and the RAC. Dealers operating the Scheme constitute a network consisting of approximately 160 Caravan Service Centres, run by the NCC's dealer network. These Caravan Service Centres are inspected regularly by the RAC and given a grading of three, four or five stars depending on the quality of the service facilities available. It is recommended that all owners should have their caravan serviced a minimum of once a year, either prior to being laid up or in the winter months before the commencement of the new season. The NCC, supported by the Caravan Club and the RAC, have recently completed a nine-month working party, looking into revamping and relaunching the Caravan Service Centre Scheme. Do make use of these excellent facilities.

Winter Storage

Rather than leaving your caravan standing in your drive or garden when not in use, you may like to think about parking it in a secure storage compound, specifically designed for caravan storage.

Many of these storage facilities exist throughout the country, some of them under cover or indoors. They are often advertised in the caravan magazines, and maybe your local caravan dealer knows of such a facility.

Security is often a first consideration, and standards vary. A storage compound will tend to be a more reliable proposition, however, than leaving your van in the front garden.

For regular visitors to the Continent, there are now frequent advertisements in the caravan press for over-wintering storage facilities in France. Also recently published are details of a Spanish storage and servicing facility at Ventallo, on the Costa Brava. The outfit is called *Caravan Inn*, and details may be obtained from them at C/Nou 25, 17472, l'Armentera (Girona) Espana, or telephone (34) 72550013. Apparently, there i always an English speaking member of staff in the office.

Checklist: Maintenance and laying up

- Rust and damp are the main enemies.

- Use grease, WD40 and Waxoyl where appropriate.

- During winter lay-up get the wheels off the ground. Better still, get them off the caravan.

- Clean the interior meticulously – no crumbs, etc should remain.

- Keep the van ventilated.

- A dehumidifier (or moisture gatherer) is well worth while.

- Leave all filler caps, etc off water containers and toilet.

- Sterilise water pipes.

- Drain water heaters against frost.

- Check external seams for dry or loose filler.

- Leave the fridge door open during lay-up, or indeed whenever the appliance is switched off.

- Have your van serviced annually by a dealer's workshop, testing gas, water and electrical systems plus chassis, brakes, couplings, etc. To save on this is false economy and potentially dangerous.

- Reseal all body seams every three or four years.

Chapter 16

Caravanning for the Disabled

Caravanning is by no means restricted to the hale and hearty. Many who are confined to wheelchairs, the partially or non-sighted, and a great number of otherwise physically handicapped people have, for years, enjoyed the freedom of caravanning.

For many this necessarily involves some sort of modification to the caravan itself, and there is a small firm of caravan builders who cater for people with such requirements. The company is called BPH Designs. They are based in Leighton Buzzard, Bedfordshire and they build 'Buzzard' caravans.

The firm is headed by Brian Hack, who told me that their prime function is that of caravan repairers. They have a comprehensively equipped workshop, capable of major caravan repair work. They are also equipped to carry out either extensive modifications to existing vans, or to build a complete caravan to the customer's specification, on a hand-built, one-off basis.

Each Buzzard caravan is unique and is built to provide for the user's special requirements. Caravans can be modified or built to cater for the very tall or the very short user, or indeed for almost any special requirement.

Wheelchair-bound caravanners are a particular case in point, and are provided for in considerable detail. Entrance and toilet doors are widened, cooking hob, sinks and washbasins are lowered, toilet layouts and beds are specially designed, and so on.

There are several firms who undertake modification of existing caravans for disabled users, but this usually stops at access ramps and widened entrance doors. BPH Designs will create a special design from the chassis upwards to cater for any individual need. Ceilings can be strengthened to take a special hoist for getting in and out of bed, and features such as the 'Caralevel' electric jacking and levelling system can be built in.

When I discussed with Brian Hack the one-off design and building service he offers, I was agreeably surprised to learn how reasonable was the cost of such a caravan. Obviously one is going to pay rather more than for a standard production model, but a bespoke 'Buzzard' is still likely to come out quite a bit cheaper than many of the well-known, hand-built conventional caravans.

It follows that the type of equipment required will dictate the final price, so this will vary. At whatever level of cost however, the service available from BPH Designs makes caravanning a practical proposition for a much wider range of handicapped people, and for many who have enjoyed conventional caravanning for some time previously, but who have become disabled in later life.

Details of the company, BPH Designs, can be found at the end of the book under 'Useful Addresses'.

A dealer who specializes in modifying existing caravans for disabled use is United British Caravans. They deal primarily in Elddis and Sprite ranges, and their workshops can carry out extensive modifications to meet a variety of disabled requirements. They have three locations, two in the Home Counties and one on Tyneside. Contact their Heathrow depot. (See Useful Addresses.)

Chapter 17

Motor Caravans

This book is essentially about caravans, but it would be incomplete without a reference to motor caravans. Motor caravanners are indeed part of the fraternity of caravanners; they are members of both the Caravan Club and the Camping and Caravanning Club. To the best of my belief they are welcome on any site, at home or abroad, where touring caravans are to be found.

There are obviously essential differences between the two, some of which give motor caravans the advantage and some which put them at a definite disadvantage.

On the plus side is compactness. By comparison with a combination of car plus caravan they take up less room, cost less to put on a ferry, are easier to drive, may legally travel faster and in many ways are more convenient. The dedicated motor caravanner could certainly extend this list of virtues.

One disadvantage is cost. Leaving out the very modest versions which are really an 8cwt commercial van with a bed and a gas stove, a comfortably appointed motor van with toilet and washing facilities, decent kitchen, fridge and so on is going to cost £16,000–£40,000 or more. For this sort of outlay one could buy a very comfortable caravan and a respectable car to tow it with.

The principal disadvantage, however, lies in its mode of use. If you are going to spend a couple of week's holiday on a campsite, every time you want to go into the town or a few miles down the coast to another beach, you have to move the whole outfit. Everything has to be packed up and stowed away before you drive off your site. (I know you can clip a pair of mopeds on the rear of the van for use at your destination, but these do lack the advantages of a car.)

That is the main disadvantage for a static holiday. If, however, you want to do a long tour around Europe, spending no more than two or three nights in one spot, a motor van wins hands down. Many retired couples, whose children have grown up and left home, cover thousands of interesting miles this way, in great comfort and with little effort. One day I may achieve my ambition to drive across the United States this way, and I would hire a 'camper' (as the Americans call a motor van).

Very great strides have been made in recent years in the design and comfort of motor vans. The earlier ones were really commercial vehicles with a couple of beds and a gas ring, and tended to be produced by commercial vehicle manufacturers. Nowadays, however, caravan manufacturers are leaving their unmistakable mark on motor homes. Firms like Swift, Elddis and Auto-Sleepers are producing vehicles which are less like commercial vans with beds and more like luxury caravans with engines. The current crop of motor caravans or motor homes are thoughtfully designed and beautifully appointed. As mentioned earlier, however, when this luxury is fitted on to, say a Mercedes chassis with a lusty engine and five-speed gearbox, the result inevitably is not cheap. It is a lot to pay for a second car, and unless you are going to live in it for a large part of each year, a second car is all you have when you get back from your holiday – and an awkward to park and cumbersome second car at that.

There is no doubt that motor caravans are a growth area. The Society of Motor Manufacturers and Traders now has a motor caravan section, and has recently formulated a Code of Practice for this specialised area. The attention to both safety and quality will be as carefully maintained and regulated as it is in the caravan manufacturing trade. Certainly their products today embody some excellent standards of design and build.

When you decide to embark on a form of nomadic self sufficiency, a motor caravan merits as much consideration as a touring caravan. The same principles apply. Consider what you can afford, to what use you want to put it, and how it would adapt to your family, your many and varied circumstances and your type of holiday.

Chapter 18

Caravanning Clubs

The Camping and Caravanning Club

One cannot write a book about caravanning without detailing the activities of the two principal clubs.

The Camping and Caravanning Club traces its origins back to 1901, and is probably the oldest organisation devoted to the interests of the nomadic holiday maker. In 1901 the Association of Cycle Campers was formed, and through the years this grew into the Club as it is today, with its four principal sections:

1   Trailer caravanners
2   Motor caravanners
3   Trailer tent campers
4   'Lightweight' campers (tent based).

The Club has a network of sites throughout the UK, where a variety of facilities are provided, most of which have mains hook-ups. All these sites are run by a warden, and full details are given in the Club's General Sites List. Many of these sites are open to non-members.

Also in the Sites List are about 2000 small sites known as 'certificated sites'. These are all in rural settings, often on farms, may only accommodate a maximum of five caravans at one time, and are strictly for members only. The more quiet and secluded of these five-van sites are known as 'hideaways'. Hideaways are clearly marked in the General Sites List, which is updated and distributed free to members every two years.

The Club also runs a system of 'temporary sites'. These are usually near popular seaside resorts, where public sites are often full at holiday times, and are organised by local units within the Club. These are available to members only.

Camping and caravanning sites overseas are listed in an annual guide produced in conjunction with the RAC. The Club is an associate of the RAC, and members may join the

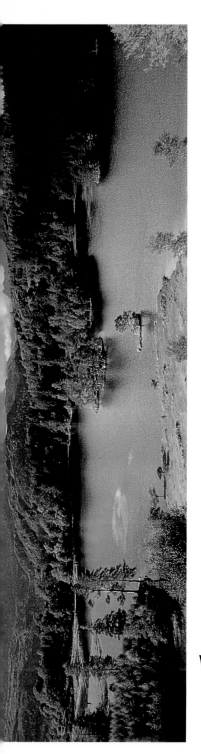

The Great Escape.

When you're making your break, get the Camping and Caravanning Club behind you. Membership gives you access to a full range of professional services, and the freedom to plan your holiday the way **you** want to.

- **Our Big Sites Book** lists almost 5,000 sites.
- **ClubCare Insurance** bureau for tents, light craft, cars and caravans.
- **Weathercall** dedicated telephone forecasting.
- **Carefree** ferry and continental touring services.
- **Club Direct** detailing our financial services . . .
- . . . All for just £27.00 (includes £4 joining fee).

RAC at preferential rates, usually about 15 per cent less than those available to the general public. The RAC Rescue and Recovery schemes are therefore available to CCC members at reduced rates. The French Federation sites guide is another most useful book which the Club can supply.

Overseas holiday arrangements can be made through the Club's 'Carefree' foreign touring service. The service takes care of ferry and continental sites bookings, the provision of International Camping Carnets, GB plates, bailbond (essential in Spain), European road maps, a useful phrasebook in several languages and so on. A comprehensive insurance package covers sickness, theft, accident and breakdown, all under the 'Get Home' service.

The Club has a nationwide network of District Associations. There are about 100 of these, grouped under 13 larger regions. Members may join their local District Association, or one of their choice further away.

In addition to these regional and district groups, there are five 'special interest' sections, namely photographic, folk dance and song, mountain activity, canoe-camping and a boating section. All these sections have a full programme of activities, and are well supported. Membership of each involves a small extra subscription to cover administration.

The Club offers insurance services for caravans, cars, motor caravans, household cover, tents and camping equipment, plus, of course, travel insurance. In addition to these services, the Club automatically covers each member for £500,000 worth of public liability.

There is a magazine circulated to members monthly which contains a good cross-section of interesting caravan-related advertisements, articles of general and technical interest, news of sites and places to visit. Foreign touring, nature con-servancy, and members' correspondence are all featured.

The Club offers an excellent technical advice service to caravanners, on all aspects of the subject. Additionally there is the 'Carascan' service, which carries out a comprehensive survey of secondhand caravans for the prospective buyer. This is available to members and non-members alike, and was mentioned at the end of Chapter 1 (Choosing a Caravan).

Finally, new members are provided with the Club's handbook, a most useful publication which describes the origins and aims of the Club, its constitution and services. Most important, it defines the various codes of conduct which campers and caravanners alike have a moral duty to adhere to. I firmly believe that all of us who use and love our countryside could do with a reminder, from time to time, of how we should behave in order not to spoil the enjoyment of others.

The Camping and Caravanning Club's current subscription is £24 plus £4 joining fee. If annual subscriptions are pledged through direct debit, the £4 joining fee is waived. This covers two adults and children under 17. The address and telephone number in Coventry can be found at the end of this book under 'Useful Addresses'.

The Caravan Club

The Caravan Club was founded about 80 years ago, and caters for the needs and interests of both trailer and motor caravanners.

In terms of membership it is the larger of the two clubs, and although many of the services provided to members are similar in each organisation, each has its own character and unique features. The two clubs complement rather than compete with each other, as do, for example the AA and the RAC. Each needs the other really, for if there were only one club, the total membership would be unwieldy, and the incentive to improve services would be gone.

The Caravan Club is based in East Grinstead, West Sussex, where a variety of specialist staff function most efficiently.

Expert technical advice is available to members on every aspect of caravanning. There is a legal department and also a Financial Plan, a personal loan service to members which operates through Frizzell Banking Services.

An ever growing and most efficient foreign touring department is a feature of the Caravan Club. Their 'Red Pennant' travel service would be hard to beat. Ferry bookings, continental site reservations, caravanning package deals, comprehensive insurance cover designed to cope with every imaginable touring misfortune, are all available on terms which compare favourably with the services of the motoring organisations. From repeated experience I can vouch for the very cheerful and courteous efficiency of the ladies in the Red Pennant travel department.

The Club publishes its members' magazine, called *En Route*, This appears eight times a year, and is a mine of interesting and practical articles, plus advertisements, correspondence and information covering the whole spectrum of caravanning.

The Club also has an insurance department which offers a wide range of cover to members. (See 'Insurance' section in Chapter 14.) In addition to the usual car and caravan holiday insurance cover, the Club offers a policy called 'Hitchfree', which is a purely personal cover for travelling abroad without either car or caravan. It can be used for either business or pleasure travelling, and is part of the 'Red Pennant' service. A most important function fulfilled by the Caravan Club is the maintaining of a computerised register of members' caravans, with chassis numbers. Police forces throughout the country make frequent use of these records when dealing with stolen caravans.

A breakdown and recovery service is available to club members, and this is run in conjunction with National Breakdown. The scheme covers motor caravans and solo cars as well as caravan outfits. It is worth noting that unlike the AA and RAC recovery schemes, the Club scheme covers the *vehicle* rather than the driver.

As the Camping and Caravanning Club has its District Associations, so the Caravan Club has its local Centres. Centres hold frequent rallies and social events all over the country, and the magazine *En Route* always has a section devoted to Centre activities. If you are attracted by the prospect of a field full of fellow caravanners from your own locality, all collected in a great gregarious gathering, drinking each other's coffee and admiring their gadgets and installations, then join your local Centre.

If peace and quiet is more your scene, then you have access, through the Club's excellent Sites Guide, to over 4000 Certificated Locations, scattered nationwide. As with the CCC Certificated Sites, these are for five vans only, and solely for members. Basic facilities and peace quiet are the usual order.

Unlike the Camping and Caravanning Club, the Caravan

Club does not have categories of membership specialising in different types of activities, but they do list Certificated Locations where various facilities and activities can be found locally. These are grouped under the headings of fishing, golf, riding and water sports (windsurfing, sailing etc). There is also a list of CLs where Bed and Breakfast is available.

These locations are listed by category of activity and geographically by county. This is a very useful feature of the Sites Directory.

The Club Sites Guide lists also the 180 or so established sites run by the Club. These are warden-controlled, have good facilities by way of toilet blocks etc and most are now equipped with mains hook-ups. A number are open all through the year, and some are open to non-members.

The Sites Guide also serves as a members' handbook and contains a remarkable amount of useful technical and legal information about caravanning and towing. It really does carry an absolute wealth of information. The Sites Guide is updated and issued free to members every two years.

Also available is a comprehensive continental sites book, which is published in two volumes. Volume One covers France, Spain, Morocco, Andorra and Portugal; Volume Two covers the rest of Europe and Scandinavia. These two books give an abundance of helpful advice on travelling abroad, varying from traffic signs to currency. We have mentioned the subject of European sites in Chapter 11. The two continental sites guides have to be purchased from the Club, but they are not expensive and are excellent value for money. The UK sites guide, as we have said, is issued free to all members.

If you are new to caravanning and are a little reluctant to tow and handle your new possession on the Queen's Highway, the Club runs a series of really helpful weekend courses on practical caravan handling and manoeuvring at various locations around the country. These are held during summer months. Details of the courses are published in *En Route*. They are also open to non-members, and details can be had from the Club.

The Club also run an increasingly popular annual event called the Caravan Club Caravanning Competition Rally (the 4Cs Rally). This is a family event, and includes a 300 mile (approx) Economy Run, a Safe Caravanning Event, an Outfit

Manoeuvring Competition, and a Concours d'Elegance. Something for everyone.

Currently, annual subscription is £26, but if you are prepared to renew by direct debit, this drops to £21. There is additional family membership at £3, which is only necessary if the rest of the family wish to use Club facilities in the absence of the named member.

If you are to get full value out of your new hobby, you really should join one of the two caravanning clubs. Their services and degree of experience will make your holidays so much easier and more enjoyable. Many caravanners are members of both clubs. Why not? The vast number of attractive locations which are exclusive to members more than justifies the small expense.

The Caravan Club details can be found at the end of the book. (See Useful Addresses.)

The National Caravan Council

We have been discussing the two caravanning clubs, whose function is to serve the interests of the caravanner. The National Caravan Council might be described as the caravan manufacturers' club. Its purpose is to coordinate and regulate the standards and practices of caravan manufacturers and their ancillary suppliers. Not so well known to caravanners as their own two clubs, the National Caravan Council is nevertheless an important and influential body, and it would be appropriate to mention it here and explain its function.

It was founded in May 1939 and reconstituted in 1953, by which time its function had clearly become to represent and coordinate all sections of the British caravan industry. Today these have fallen into four main groups, the caravan manufacturers, the dealers who trade in caravans, the many companies who supply the manufacturers and dealers with their goods, accessories and services, and finally the owners and operators of caravan sites and parks. Each of these sections is represented on the governing committee of the Council, and there are numerous sub-committees which deal with specialist sections of the whole spectrum of caravanning.

What has all this got to do with me, you ask. Well, quite a

lot really. The ultimate beneficiary of the National Caravan Council's many activities is you, the end user, the actual caravanner. Caravans become more and more sophisticated, more technical, as time goes on. The exacting standards, the British Standard Specifications to which all these* complicated accessories are made, including the chassis and shell of the caravan itself, all these standards of quality and safety are the work of the National Caravan Council and its expert technical section.

The NCC coordinates the activities of all the many concerns which make up the caravan industry, and all this in the interests of the caravanner. You will find many references to the NCC in this book, and the point is made more than once that any caravanner is welcome to approach the National Caravan Council, if there is a problem which cannot be solved by a dealer. The NCC is based in Aldershot, and the address and telephone number can be found in the 'Useful Addresses' section at the end of the book.

Chapter 19

To Sum Up

That's about it really. I have tried to avoid being too technical and by no means have I covered the subject comprehensively. The object was to produce a guide to some of the aspects of caravanning, which might bewilder a newcomer but which an older hand might find useful and of interest.

In common with motoring, sailing or photography, to name only a few popular activities, caravanning is something in which you can just as easily dabble or become deeply involved. As with the other three subjects, you can certainly spend a lot of money although this is by no means essential. Simple, uncomplicated equipment is readily available. You can see an elderly van, on which loving care is obviously spent, being towed behind a modest family car, and you can see a more ambitious model following a Mercedes or a Jaguar; one usually finds there is a fellowship among caravanners that cuts right across the value or opulence of the equipment.

Certainly, as with our examples of motoring, sailing and photography, you can get very technical indeed, although this is in no way necessary in order to enjoy the hobby. As a source of technical advice and information, you cannot do better than the Caravan Club. It has a wealth of informative leaflets on the many aspects of caravanning and, if there is no leaflet, will gladly supply you with any help or information on your own particular problem. Using a caravan without joining the Caravan Club is rather like going to a concert wearing ear plugs. The National Caravan Council also are always only too willing to give advice and assistance.

Epilogue

On the South Cornish coast is a small, rather remote village which we will call Porthfallow. Just outside the village is Arthur's farm. This consists of a cottage with no mains services whatsoever, and a few fields which slope gently down to the cliff top. From there a short path leads down to a rocky beach. The view from the fields is breathtaking, and the peace is indescribable.

We first met Arthur many years ago when our children were small. He has made a comfortable living from families who have camped and caravanned in his fields. At our first meeting Arthur wore a tweed cap and jacket of indeterminable pattern, corduroy trousers and wellies. He wears these same items to this day, in hot or cold weather alike. He doesn't say a lot, he

has a simple philosophy and is good company. Both Arthur and his cottage look as though they have been there for about 200 years.

Nowadays one camps either in the pasture or the 'medder' – not much to choose between them. Each has the same superb view of the cliff top, the sweeping bay and the sea. Each boasts one water tap, and the sanitary essentials are in the pasture. Here Arthur gets a gent with a JCB to dig a pit at the beginning of the season, with back-fill and shovel left handily alongside. Toilets are emptied here and by the end of the summer it's about filled in.

We have caravanned with our young family over the years in Arthur's 'medder' and in sites at home and abroad. These have ranged from the very basic up to sites with swimming pools, bars, discos, take-aways and so on. We have served our time through the trauma of the school holiday travel, and crowded roads and ferries, but the youngsters are now all self-supporting, thankfully, and we can please ourselves. We can steal away in June or at the end of September or even both. We have graduated! Caravanning now in our comfortable two-berth Herself, me and Polly, our retriever, who has got caravanning down to a fine art.

We both love Brittany and the French people, the sunshine and the atmosphere of the well-run continental campsites. To me, though, the essence of caravanning is a weekend at our favourite and mostly deserted location in Derbyshire. Better still is the evening of an Indian summer in early October in Arthur's 'medder' with a glass of ale at hand and the mind in neutral. Children are back at school, all the people in funny hats have gone home, and Porthfallow returns to normal for the rest of the year. (I'm told that sex and cider constitute the principal recreation in Porthfallow of a winter and come to that there's not much more to do in the summer.)

If the bright lights are not for you, then I hope you find your own Porthfallow. I'm certainly not telling you where ours is.

Go safely and enjoy your freedom.

Useful Addresses

Associations

Camping and Caravan Club
Greenfields House
Westwood Way
Coventry CV4 8JH
0203 694995
Carascan
Carefree contact the Camping and Caravanning Club

Caravan Club
East Grinstead House
East Grinstead
West Sussex RH19 1UA
0342 326994
Caracheck
Mayday contact the Caravan Club

National Caravan Council
Catherine House
Victoria Road
Aldershot
Hampshire GU11 1SS
0252 318251

Royal Automobile Club (RAC)
For local office, see your telephone directory

The Forestry Commission
Forest Holidays
231 Corstorphine Road
Edinburgh EH12 7AT
031-334 0303 or 2567

National Park Authorities

Brecon Beacons National Park
Glamorgan Street
Brecon
Powys LD3 7DP

Dartmoor National Park
Devon County Council
County Hall
Exeter
Devon

Exmoor National Park
Exmoor House
Dulverton
Somerset TA22 9HL

Lake District National Park
County Hall
Kendal
Cumbria

Northumberland National Park
Bede House
All Saints Centre
Newcastle-upon-Tyne NE1 2DH

North Yorkshire Moors National Park
The Old Vicarage
Bondgate
Helmsley
Yorkshire YO6 5BP

Peak District National Park
Aldern House
Baslow Road
Bakewell
Derbyshire DE4 1AE

Pembrokeshire Coast National Park
County Offices
Haverfordwest
Dyfed

Snowdonia National Park
Penrhyndendraeth
Gwynedd LL48 4LS

Yorkshire Dales National Park
Yorebridge
Bainbridge
Leyburn
North Yorkshire

Accessories Manufacturers

AFS Engineering
Firsdale Industrial Estate
Units 4 and 5
Nangreave Street
Leigh
Lancs WN7 4TN
0942 261 899

General accessories, including stabilizers and car plates

Bicknacre Caravan and Leisure
39 Peartree Lane
Bicknacre
Essex CM3 4LS
0245 225761

Elgena range electric water heaters

BPH Designs
109 Heath Road
Leighton Buzzard
Beds LU7 8AD
0525 371645

Touring caravans, comprehensively equipped
and made to customers' individual specifications

Calor Gas Ltd
Riding Court Road
Slough
Bucks SL3 9JG
0753 540000
(or see telephone directory
for local depot)

Carver & Co (Engineers) Ltd
Engine Lane
Coppice Side Industrial Estate
Brownhills
Walsall WS8 7ES
0543 452122

Space heaters, water heaters and pump systems

Gaslow (Grade (UK) Ltd)
5 Factory Lane
Beeston
Nottingham NG9 4AB
0602 259646

Omnidirectional TV aerial, Gaslow gauge (gas level indicator
which checks system for leaks)

Gobur Caravans
Peacock Way
Melton Constable
Norfolk NR24 2BY
0263 860031

Carousel range of folding caravans

Grove Products (Caravan Accessories Ltd)
Unit 7, National Industrial Estate
Richmond Street
Ashton-Under-Lyme
Lancs OL7 0AU
061-344 2306

Wholesalers of wide range of caravan accessories

Harrier Designs
Longsleddale
Woodside Avenue
Lymington
Hampshire SO41 8FG
0590 6787471

Pozilok (safety device for wheel protection)

Hella Ltd
Wildmere Industrial Estate
Banbury
Oxon OX16 7JU
0295 272233

Electrical supplies and towing kits

Isabella International Camping Ltd
Isabella House
Thame Station Industrial Park
Thame
Oxon OX9 3UH
0844 261711

Isabella awnings and their accessories

J K Products
Unit No 22
Parkwood Drive
Rawtenstall
Lancs BB4 6RP
0706 217221

The Vanguard Stand (protects caravan wheels while in storage)

Lionweld Kennedy Ltd
Marsh Road
Middlesbrough
Cleveland TS1 5JS
0642 245151

Wheel clamps

Mobile Homes Insurance Service
4 Augusta Place
Leamington CV32 5EL
0926 452626

New Concept
PO Box 61
Winchester
Hants SO23 8XR
0962 840769

Easylift Air Jack

Safe and Secure Products
Chestnut House
Chesley Hill
Wick
Bristol BS15 5NE
0272 564908

Security locks and alarms

Selsmore (Marketing) Ltd
Unit 23
The Tanneries
Brockhampton Lane
Havant
Hants PO9 1JB
0705 492907

Lambilevel (caravan leveller)

Strawson Inclinometers Ltd
3A Thornhill Industrial Estate
Rotherham S60 1LH
0709 367969

Levelling instruments

Thetford Ltd
Centrovell Industrial Estate
Caldwell Road
Nuneaton
Warwicks CV11 4UD
0203 341941

Portable and fitted toilets

United British Caravans
Colnbrook By-Pass (A4)
West Drayton
Middlesex UB7 0HE
0753 682606

Caravan conversions for the disabled

W4 Ltd
Ford Lane Industrial Estate
Arundel
West Sussex BM18 0DF
0243 553355

Anti-theft devices and nose weight scales

C P Witter Ltd
18 Canal Side
Chester CH1 3LL
0244 341166

Towbars

A COMPLETE RANGE OF THETFORD PORTA POTTIS

Thetford is the world's leading portable toilet manufacturer providing a full range of Porta Pottis to suit all types and sizes of caravan, camping car, tent trailer, small boat and holiday chalet. Thetford Porta Pottis are also suitable for domestic use, in the attic or bedroom, where no other personal toilet facilities exist. Thetford portable toilets are built from advanced and high quality plastic and represent the most ideal and hygienic form of personal sanitation you can buy.

THE INTEGRATED POUR OUT SPOUT SYSTEM

In addition to their high-quality and durability, all Thetford portable fresh water flushing toilets have one important thing in common - the unique Thetford integrated pour out spout system.

This unique innovation, combined with other exclusive features, ensures that the Thetford Porta Potti waste tank can be emptied cleanly and with ease. When the waste tank level indicator is fully red, it's time to empty the waste holding tank. Operating the quick release lever takes apart the portable toilet and the waste tank can be carried to an appropriate location. With just a twist of the wrist, the integrated pour out spout can be swivelled upwards and its cap removed. Then, with a thumb on the vacuum release button, the waste can be poured out easily and without splashing. A special valve handle lock prevents accidental spillage from the waste tank itself during emptying.

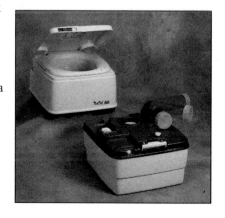

THE THETFORD CASSETTE PORTA POTTI
MAXIMUM COMFORT AND HYGIENE

The Thetford Cassette Porta Potti has been designed
to form an integral and permanent part of
caravan and motorhome bathrooms and
provides a high level of convenience and
luxury. The built-in Cassette toilet,
complete with toilet-tissue holder and
waste level indicator, has a portable waste
disposal system which allows everything
to do with emptying and preparation of
the toilet to take place <u>outside</u> the caravan.
So the comfort and lifestyle inside the
vehicle is never disturbed.

THETFORD AQUA PRODUCTS

Thetford Aqua Products ensure the efficient operation and longer life of
Thetford Porta Pottis and Cassette Porta Pottis.

AQUA KEM concentrate is a thick,
non-drip toilet fluid with a very low
cost per dosage. Pleasantly perfumed
and biodegradeble, it prevents odour
build up, helps dissolve waste matter
and keeps the holding tank clean.
AQUA KEM GREEN is a non-toxic
and formaldehyde-free toilet fluid
which is also concentrated and highly effective. It does not irritate eyes or
skin and is ecologically and environmentally friendly. AQUA KEM
GREEN has been completely tested to OECD (EEC) safety standards.
AQUA RINSE is an important flush water additive which cleans and protects the bowl at the same time as it improves the effectiveness of flushing.
AQUA SOFT is a special tissue which flushes easily from the toilet bowl
and dissolves rapidly in the waste holding tank preventing clogs.
As the world's leading manufacturer of sanitation products for the
recreational area, Thetford is committed to the continual development of
effective and environment-friendly toilet fluids.

Thetford Ltd.
Centrovell Industrial Estate
Caldwell Road, Nuneaton
Warwickshire, CV 11 4UD
Tel.: 0203-341941
Fax: 0203-641230

WHERE ALL THE GREAT IDEAS COME FROM

THETF✦RD

Index of Advertisers